CW00746762

On
Baptismal Fonts:
Ancient and Modern

by S. Anita Stauffer

Study Secretary for Worship and Congregational Life
Lutheran World Federation, Geneva, Switzerland

THE ALCUIN CLUB and the GROUP FOR RENEWAL OF WORSHIP (GROW)

The Alcuin Club, which exists to promote the study of Christian liturgy in general and of Anglican liturgy in particular, traditionally published a single volume annually for its members. This ceased in 1986 but resumed in 1992. Similarly, GROW was responsible from 1975 to 1986 for the quarterly 'Grove Liturgical Studies'. Since the beginning of 1987 the two have sponsored a Joint Editorial Board to produce quarterly 'Joint Liturgical Studies', details of which are to be found at the end of this Study.

THE COVER PHOTOGRAPH

shows the fifth-century cruciform font, now partially filled in, in Thuburbo Majus, Tunisia. (See chapter 3)

First Impression September 1994
ISSN 0951-2667
ISBN 1 85174 276 X

GROVE BOOKS LIMITED
Bramcote   Nottingham   NG9 3DS

CONTENTS

ILLUSTRATION CREDITS

Unless otherwise indicated, all photographs are by the author. Gratitude is expressed to those who provided photographs, plans, and permissions.

Chapter 4: 1. Photo courtesy of Belli & Belli, Architects; 4. Photo copyright Richard Sexton, courtesy of Mighetto Goldin, Architects; 5. Photo by Robin Coutts, courtesy of David Stancliffe; 7. Plan courtesy of John C. Voosen, Architects; 8. Plan courtesy of Belli & Belli, Architects; 9. Photo courtesy of David Housholder; 10. Photo courtesy of Alan Fudge.

Colour Plates: 1. Photo by the author, published by permission of B. Younes Habib, Conservateur du Musée National du Bardo, Tunis; 4. Courtesy of David Housholder.

Preface

This little book has a modest definition: it is a report of research in progress, in an attempt to understand the meaning and practice of baptism in the early Church and to renew its practice in liturgical churches today. The primary focus of the research is ancient and modern baptismal fonts, because these *places* of baptism have too often been ignored by liturgical historians and liturgists. A thorough examination of baptism (in history or today) cannot even be approached without attending to the archaeological, architectural, liturgical, and theological evidence these fonts present.

Chapter 1 examines the meaning and modes of baptism, and chapter 2 gives an overview of the history and meaning of fonts. In chapter 3, nearly fifty early Christian fonts are introduced, as a means of illustrating the richness of baptism in the patristic Church and, in a sense, to suggest some prototypes for fonts today. Chapter 4 is an attempt to provide, on the foundations of the historical explorations, architectural and ritual suggestions for recovering baptism's rich meanings in liturgical churches today. The point is not repristination, but renewal of the life of the Church.

There are intentional limitations to the historical material in this volume. First, it concentrates in the West.[1] Second, it deals with fonts, and only incidentally with the baptisteries which were their spatial context.[2] Third, it is limited to fonts which I have examined personally.[3] Fourth, it focuses on the water bath of baptism, and is not concerned with other ritual elements. Fifth, it is written for those without training in early Christian archaeology. Sixth, it must acknowledge that there are unanswered questions about many of the historical sites, because of physical damage, or because re-excavation is needed, or because liturgical texts are lacking. As excavating continues, some questions will be answered, and some conclusions here will change. Some of the questions will never be answered.

Where possible, translations of patristic writings have been quoted from readily accessible sources, to encourage readers to pursue the writings.

Citations in footnotes are abbreviated; full information is provided in the bibliography.

With a grateful heart I thank those who have shared knowledge and explored questions with me: Ralph R. Van Loon (who reviewed chapter 4), Edward J. Yarnold, S.J., (who reviewed my manuscript); and Mario Mirabella Roberti, Richard Krautheimer, Noel Duval, Eugene L. Brand and Gordon Lathrop, all of whose writings and consultations have given me insight. I acknowledge a similar debt to the late J. G. Davies. Finally, I thank Margaret A. Alexander, who with generous graciousness has both literally and figuratively opened to me the baptisteries of ancient Tunisia, and who has insightfully reviewed my manuscript; it is to her that I dedicate this book.

---

[1] Dura-Europos, Syria, is the exception. It is included because it is by far the most ancient font discovered by archaeologists.

[2] Prior literature has given predominant attention to the baptisteries, often virtually ignoring the fonts—their *raison d'être!*

[3] With the exception of Dura-Europos.

1. Water and Baptism

In the beginning was the primeval water of chaos. In the end will be the river of the water of life. Between creation and the eschaton, human beings are formed in the waters of their mothers' wombs, and life is sustained by water. It is an absolute necessity; there cannot be life on earth without water. In situations of inadequate water, humans as well as plants and animals eventually die.

But water is multivalent; it is death-dealing as well as life-giving. In water there is both creation and destruction, both life and death. When there is too much of it, water can be an agent of destruction. In torrential rains and floods, people are drowned, trees are uprooted, and property is obliterated.

A third layer of meaning to water comes from its use in washing and bathing. In human use, bathing is both cleansing and renewing. A look at the monumental public baths of the ancient Roman world makes it clear that even then bathing was for purposes beyond the hygienic, although that was and is primary.

Not only is water both creative and destructive in nature, and cleansing in human life, but also in its uses by its Creator. The waters of creation in Genesis come to their culmination in the river of the water of life in Paradise described in Revelation (22.1-2). God used water in the great Flood both to destroy the face of the earth, and to save Noah and his family. Likewise, God parted the waters of the Red Sea to save the Israelites, then caused the returning waves to drown the Egyptians and all the Pharaoh's horses. Repeatedly in the Bible, purification from sin is described as washing. Most importantly, Jesus himself is the living water (John 4.10).

Here, in brief, are the phenomenological and typological bases for some of the principal meanings of water in holy baptism. Like water itself, baptism is also about birth/life, death/burial, and bath. There are other layers of meaning to baptism, of course, but these are the principal meanings related to the symbolism of water. Such typology was often reflected in ancient prayers over the water for baptism, and, following this tradition, the typological understanding of water was fully reflected by Martin Luther in the 'flood prayer' (*Sintflutgebet*) of his 1523 baptismal rite:

> 'Almighty eternal God, according to your righteous judgment you condemned the unbelieving world through the flood, and in your great mercy you preserved Noah and his family. You drowned hard-hearted Pharaoh and his host in the Red Sea and led your people Israel through the same on dry ground, thereby prefiguring this bath of baptism. Through the baptism of your dear Child, our Lord Jesus Christ, you have consecrated and set apart the Jordan and all water as a salutary flood and a rich and full washing away of sins . . .'[1]

---

[1] Translation based on that in Ulrich S. Leupold, (ed.), *Luther's Works: Liturgy and Hymns*, Vol. 53 (Fortress Press, Philadelphia, 1965), p.97. This prayer was not original with Luther, but was his adaptation of tradition as he knew it. Luther's prayer was adopted by Thomas Cranmer in his 1549 baptismal rite; these medieval prayers are the
[continued on p.7 opposite]

MEANINGS OF BAPTISM

These several layers of the meaning of water are reflected in the theology of baptism and the symbolism of the baptismal font. Birth and cleansing seem to have been the most prominent understandings of baptism in the West prior to the fourth century, when the paschal understanding of baptism gained prominence.[1] Birth imagery for baptism is predominant in the East, but there are mentions of it also in the West. The primary biblical foundation for this understanding is John 3.5, 'No one can enter the kingdom of God without being born of water and Spirit.' In Titus 3.5, baptism is referred to as 'the water of rebirth and renewal by the Holy Spirit.' In the late second century, Irenaeus of Lyon referred to the baptismal font as a womb.[2]

In early third-century Carthage, North Africa (in what is now Tunisia), Tertullian wrote extensively of baptism as birth, and he described the baptized as 'little fish' who begin their life in the water and who cannot survive except by remaining 'in the water' with Christ, the 'great Fish'[3]; indeed, Tertullian's emphasis on water is dramatized by his contrast between fish, which can only live in water, and vipers, asps, and other serpents, which live in dry and waterless places.[4] Fish imagery was also used by Ambrose, two centuries later in Milan. After referring to the living creatures in the waters of creation, he said to the newly baptized:

'These were born in the beginning, at the creation; but this gift was kept for you: that the waters should regenerate you into grace, even as those other waters generated into life. Imitate the fish; it received a lesser grace than you, but you should still consider it a marvel. It is in the sea and above the waves . . . On the sea the tempest rages, violent winds blow; but the fish swims on. It does not drown because it is used to swimming. In the same way, this world is the sea for you. It has various currents, huge waves, fierce storms. You too must be a fish, so that the waves of this world do not drown you.'[5]

---

primary sources for prayers over the water in the American *Lutheran Book of Worship* (1978), the American Episcopal *Book of Common Prayer* (1979), the Church of England *Alternative Service Book* (1980), the Canadian Anglican *Book of Alternative Services* (1985), the Anglican *A New Zealand Prayer Book* (1989), the South African *Anglican Prayer Book* (1989), and the American Methodist *Book of Common Worship* (1993). A similar prayer is also used in the contemporary Roman Catholic baptismal rite.

[1] Kavanagh (1978), p.46. For biblical and patristic background on the symbolism of the font as tomb and womb, see Bedard and Riley. Similar, although less focused, information is provided in Burnish.

[2] *Adversus haereses* 4.

[3] It is interesting to note that there is a pavement mosaic from an early third-century Christian catacomb in Hadrumetum (now known as Sousse, Tunisia) which presents this idea with marine iconography. A dolphin in the centre represents the crucified Christ. An anchor replaces the cross, conflating baptism and crucifixion. The small fish represent baptized Christians. Additionally, a multitude of fish are depicted in mosaic on the surface of the late-sixth-century font from Kélibia, Tunisia (see chapter 3).

[4] *De Baptismo* 1.

[5] *De Sacramentis* III:3; English text in Yarnold, p. 121 (2nd ed., p.121).

Tertullian's birth imagery was picked up later by other North Africans, including Cyprian, Optatus, and Augustine. In north-eastern Italy in the mid-fourth century, Zeno of Verona (but who was born in Africa) wrote of the baptismal font as the womb of the virgin mother, the Church.[1] Such font-as-womb imagery was also used in North Africa by Augustine and Quodvultdeus. In late fourth-century Milan, Ambrose, whose principal understanding of baptism was paschal, also referred to baptism as 'entering . . . mother's womb and being born again.'[2] In Rome in the mid-fifth century, Leo the Great also called baptism a birth and the font a womb.[3]

Baptism is also a bath, a washing (1 Corinthians 6.11; Ephesians 5.26; 2 Peter 1.9), a sacramental purification from sin. In mid-second-century Rome, Justin described baptism as a washing.[4] Half a century later in Carthage, Tertullian made it clear that this is no ordinary bath, however: 'The flesh is washed that the soul may be made spotless.'[5] Later in the third century, Cyprian of Carthage also wrote of baptism as washing, adding that 'the water ought to be first cleansed and sanctified by the bishop that it may be able to wash away in its baptism the sins of the man who is baptized.'[6] In the eighth-century Gallo-Roman Gelasian Sacramentary, the prayer consecrating the font calls it an 'unspotted womb', but then switches to bath imagery:

'May the fount be alive, the water regenerating, the wave purifying, so that all who shall be washed in this saving laver by the operation of the Holy Spirit within them may be brought to the mercy of perfect cleansing.'[7]

But by the fourth century, the predominant understanding of baptism, especially in the West, was paschal: to be baptized is to be joined to the death and resurrection of Christ (Romans 6.3-5; Colossians 2.12). The three meanings— birth, bath, burial—are not unrelated, however. The baptismal bath is in fact a drowning flood (1 Peter 3.20-21); the new birth must be preceded by the death of the old person. As St. Paul wrote:

'Do you not know that all of us who have been baptized into Christ Jesus were baptized into his death? Therefore we have been buried with him by baptism into death, so that, just as Christ was raised from the dead by the glory of the Father, so we too might walk in newness of life.' (Romans 6.3-5; NRSV)

Already in third-century Egypt, Origen had reflected Romans 6 in writing of baptism[8] and had referred to the font as a sepulchre[9], but the paschal understanding became the *cantus firmus* in the fourth-century mystagogical

---

[1] *Invitations to the Baptismal Font* IV.
[2] *De mysteriis* IX:59; English text in Srawley, p.151.
[3] For examples, see *Sermones* 24, *In nativitatem Domini*; 25, *In nativitate Domini*; and 70, *De passione Domini*.
[4] *First Apology* 61.
[5] *De Resurrectione Carnis* 8; English text in Whitaker, p.10.
[6] Letter 70, to Januarius, 1; English text in Finn, p.138.
[7] Book I:XLIV; Whitaker, p.187.
[8] *Homily on Exodus* 5:2.
[9] *In Romanos* 5:8.

writings of Cyril of Jerusalem, Chrysostom, Theodore of Mopsuestia, and Ambrose. In late fourth-century Milan, Ambrose said to his neophytes, 'Because you are immersed, the sentence, "You are dust and to dust you shall return", is served . . . So it is that the font is a kind of grave.'[1] He elaborated, '. . . you were immersed: which means that you were buried with Christ.'[2] A few decades later in North Africa, Augustine (who had been baptized in Milan by Ambrose) combined the birth and paschal images of baptism: 'All who attain to this grace die thereby to sin . . . and they are thereby alive by being reborn in the baptismal font, just as Christ rose again from the sepulchre.'[3] Also in the fourth century, Cyril of Jerusalem combined the motifs of birth and death. Speaking to neophytes of their triple submersion, Cyril commented:

'In one and the same action you died and were born; the water of salvation became both tomb and mother for you . . . A single moment achieves both ends, and your begetting was simultaneous with your death.'[4]

In the mid-fifth century, Pope Leo the Great, defending the practice of baptism at the Easter Vigil, wrote, 'in the rite of baptism death comes from the slaying of sin, and the triple immersion imitates the three days of burial, and the rising out of the water is like his rising from the tomb.'[5]

This baptismal resurrection into new life in Christ has an eschatological note: it is proleptic entrance into Paradise.[6] While this understanding of baptism is stronger in the East[7] than in the West, it is not absent in the West. In the third century in Carthage, Cyprian wrote:

'The Church, setting forth the likeness of paradise, includes within her four walls fruit-bearing trees . . . These trees she waters with four rivers, that is, with the four Gospels, wherewith, by a celestial inundation, she bestows the grace of saving Baptism.'[8]

MODES OF BAPTISM

Four terms have been used to designate the various modes of baptism: submersion, immersion, affusion, and aspersion. About the first two there has been unending confusion and debate.

Submersion is sometimes called 'total immersion', thus referring to the fact that in submersion a person's entire body is pushed completely under the water. Another common English term for this mode is 'dipping'. Symbolically and experientially, submersion is the fullest representation of the paschal meaning of

---

[1] *De Sacramentis* II:19; Yarnold, p.117 (2nd ed., p.113).
[2] *De Sacramentis* II:20; Yarnold, p.117 (2nd ed., p.118).
[3] *Enchiridion* 8:42; Finn, p.152.
[4] *Mystagogic Catecheses*, Sermon 2:4; Yarnold, p.76 (2nd ed., p.78).
[5] *Epistle 16*; Finn, p.81.
[6] See Stauffer, 'Fonts: Baptism, Pascha, and Paradise'.
[7] A particularly rich example is Ode 11 of the *Odes of Solomon*, from second-century East Syria. See the translation by James Charlesworth, quoted in Thomas M. Finn, *Early Christian Baptism and the Catechumenate: West and East Syria* (Liturgical Press, Collegeville, Minnesota, 1992), pp.117-118.
[8] *Epistle* 72:10; translation in Alexander Roberts and James Donaldson, (eds.), *The Ante-Nicene Fathers*, Volume V (Charles Scribner's Sons, New York, 1925), p.382.

baptism. To be submersed is to be buried under the water; it is (almost) to drown. Submersion is also an effective act of new birth, as the candidate comes up out of the water as out of the womb. Submersion is also the most complete ritual act of baptism as cleansing. For submersion to be practised, the water must be quite deep. (See chapter 4 regarding the practice of submersion.)

In *immersion*, the adult candidate stands or kneels in water (usually of a depth between the ankles and the waist) while water is poured over the head, or the head is pushed *partially* into the water. With an infant, the body (especially the head) is lowered partially into the water, or the body is partially lowered into the water as water is poured over the head. Immersion is not as full a sign of any of baptism's meanings as is submersion.

It is not known how Jesus was baptized, though the most ancient artistic representations show immersion, not submersion. It is also not known how Baptism in apostolic and post-apostolic times was done. The earliest fonts in the West, in the third and fourth centuries, were often not deep enough for easy submersion. By the fifth and sixth centuries, some fonts were deep enough for submersion, although it is not known in most places whether submersion was actually practised.

Part of the confusion between submersion and immersion is that in many ancient texts in the West, it is difficult or impossible to determine which mode was meant. Then the archaeological evidence is crucial, but unfortunately in many places it has been wholly or partially destroyed. In addition to knowing the size and depth of the font, it is necessary to know the water source and whether there was a drain. In the absence of such evidence, it is simply impossible to know where submersion was used, and where immersion was used. It is clear, however, from both texts and archaeology, that in baptism in the patristic and early medieval periods an abundant amount of water was normally used.

Affusion is a mode in which water is poured over the candidate's head. Affusion began to replace immersion, especially in cold northern countries, as the baptism of infants became common in the Middle Ages. According to J. G. Davies, by the fourteenth century affusion was common in France, while it did not become widespread in Italy until the fifteenth century, nor in England until the sixteenth.[1] Martin Luther encouraged a return to submersion in sixteenth-century Germany, as a more complete sign of the radical paschal meaning of baptism.[2] Likewise the Church of England's 1549, 1552, and 1662 Prayer Books also called for dipping. However, it was not until the late twentieth century that congregations of liturgical churches have begun once again practising either submersion or immersion.

Aspersion, or sprinkling, is the most minimal mode of baptism. Prior to the late Middle Ages, it was used only in clinical baptisms (that is, of dying persons, for which Cyprian of Carthage defended the practice.[1] However, sprinkling was the

---

[1] *The Architectural Setting of Baptism*, p.73.
[2] See his *Large Catechism*, section on Baptism; 'The Holy and Blessed Sacrament of Baptism' (1519), *Luther's Works*, Vol. 35 (Fortress Press, Philadelphia, 1960), p.29; 'The Babylonian Captivity of the Church' (1520), *Luther's Works*, Vol. 36 (Fortress Press, Philadelphia, 1959), pp.67-68; and Luther's 1523 baptismal rite, *Luther's Works*, Vol. 53 (Fortress Press, Philadelphia, 1965), p.100.

which Cyprian of Carthage defended the practice.[1] However, sprinkling was the normal parish practice by the Renaissance, and fonts had become tiny. The result was a minimalistic understanding of baptism. Renewed baptismal rites in the late twentieth century have called for a more abundant use of water, and have often suggested submersion or at least immersion. The landmark ecumenical document, *Baptism, Eucharist and Ministry*, said clearly that 'In the celebration of baptism the symbolic dimension of water should be taken seriously and not minimalized.'[2]

MOVEMENT IN THE RITUAL

Fonts are containers designed to hold the water in which baptism is administered. In addition to the mode of baptism, two other movements in the water are important with regard to the design of fonts. These movements are the twin actions of descent/ascent, and the act of passage through the water. All three have symbolic meanings.

The earliest baptisteries in the West, in Rome and Milan, had in-ground pools with steps. The steps were not merely utilitarian; indeed, sometimes the early fonts were so shallow that steps were not even actually necessary. It would seem that the steps were installed for symbolic purposes: in order for the candidate to experience descent into burial with Christ, and ascent into new life in the resurrection. Ambrose and other patristic writers referred frequently to 'going down' into the water. It is possible to conceptualize the meanings of baptism in this period in terms of descent from the world and ascent into the body of Christ.[3] In time the number of steps was interpreted symbolically.

The experience of passage through the waters was also important in the patristic period, no doubt a reference to the passage of the Israelites through the Red Sea. Ambrose wrote:

'He who passes through the waters of this font—that is, from earthly things to heavenly (for this is the meaning of this passage, this pasch: it is the passage of the person who is baptized; it is a passage from sin to life, from guilt to grace, from vileness to holiness—he who passes through these waters does not die; he rises again.'[4]

Most paleo-Christian fonts in the West had steps on at least two sides, perhaps enabling the candidate to experience passage through the water from the old life to the new.

---

[1] Letter 69: 12.
[2] Faith and Order Paper No. 111 (World Council of Churches, Geneva, 1982), Baptism V.18, p.6.
[3] See schematic in Wayne A. Meeks, *The First Urban Christians* (Yale University Press, New Haven, Connecticut, 1983) p.156.
[4] *De Sacramentis* I:12; Yarnold, p.104 (2nd ed., pp.104-105).

2. Baptismal Space

Baptism is by water and the Spirit (John 3.5). While the Holy Spirit can be anywhere and everywhere, water needs a *place* to be, a container. In nature, of course, water's containers are oceans and seas, lakes and ponds, streams and rivers. It was in those large natural water 'vessels' that Christian baptisms first occurred. Jesus was baptized in the River Jordan. Most other New Testament accounts of baptisms do not indicate where they took place. The baptism of the Ethiopian eunuch by Philip happened simply when they 'came to some water,' and the two 'went down into the water,' where Philip baptized him (Acts 8.36-8). In Acts 16.13-15, probably Lydia and her family were baptized in a river outside a gate to Philippi (in what is now Greece).

Just as the writers of the New Testament seem to have assumed that baptisms would be done in natural bodies of water and thus did not exert much effort in describing the places, so too in post-apostolic times. In the first two or three centuries of Christianity, the usual sites for baptism were also natural bodies of water: streams, rivers, lakes, and the sea. The *Didache*, a church manual probably written in Syria sometime between A.D. 60 and A.D. 160[1], said that baptism in the Triune Name is to happen 'in running water,' but added that, if there is no running water, 'other water' could be used, and if there was neither, water could be poured.[2] The text added that cold water was better than warm.

In Rome in about A.D. 160, the *First Apology* of Justin Martyr indicated simply that baptism occurred 'where there is water'.[3]

Approximately A.D. 215, in Rome, the *Apostolic Tradition* attributed to Hippolytus[4] specified that the water should be 'pure and flowing'[5]. The presbyter was to stand 'at the water', as the deacon and candidate went 'down . . . into the water'.[6] It is not known whether this was in a natural body of water or perhaps in a pool in a building or courtyard.

In Carthage, North Africa, sometime between A.D. 160-220, Tertullian wrote that it 'makes no difference' whether baptism happens 'in a sea or a pool, a stream or a fount, a lake or a trough . . .'[7] Here, then, is acknowledgment that both natural bodies of water and constructed pools were being used for baptism. As early as the second century, while there were persecutions, sometimes baptism may have occurred in the baths and courtyard fountains of private homes and perhaps in small public baths.[8]

---

[1] The *Didache* was perhaps a redacted text by multiple people at different times.
[2] Chapter 7; Whitaker, p.1.
[3] 61; Whitaker, p.2.
[4] It is not known whether *Apostolic Tradition* was describing actual baptismal practice in Rome, or what its author considered to be the ideal.
[5] XXI:2; Whitaker, p.5.
[6] XXI:11; Whitaker, p.5.
[7] *On Baptism* 4; text in Alexander Roberts and James Donaldson, (eds.), *The Ante-Nicene Fathers*, III (Charles Scribner's Sons, New York, 1918), pp.670-671.
[8] Krautheimer (1986), p.24.

The oldest archaeological evidence of a baptismal font *per se* is in the mid-third-century house church in Dura-Europos, in what is now Syria. The font is rectangular, which seems to have been the normal shape of the most ancient fonts.[1] In the fourth century, particularly after the Roman Emperor Constantine ended the persecutions in A.D. 313, special places for Baptism were constructed or adapted. During that period, adult baptism was the norm. To accommodate all of the candidates for baptism, and to provide privacy, since they were baptized naked, the baptisteries in the West were usually detached or only loosely attached to the church buildings. The fonts were in-ground pools. The earliest and most important baptisteries in the West were in Rome (where the most ancient font was round) and Milan (with octagonal fonts). Through the sixth and into the seventh century, fonts were almost always built in the ground. The sense of descent into and ascent out of the water was important in both theology and practice. A variety of shapes occurred, with geographical differences. For example, in Italy and France, octagonal and hexagonal fonts were most common. In early Christian Tunisia, there were many cruciform and quatrilobe fonts, as well as hexagonal ones. Circular and other shapes of fonts were found in a variety of places.

In early centuries after Constantine, baptisteries in the West were located in cathedrals, since the bishops presided at baptisms. However, as the Church grew, there were not enough bishops to accommodate all the catechumens, and presbyters of parishes were permitted to administer the water bath (though not the consignation, and hence the beginning of the separation of baptism from confirmation[2]). As a result, baptisteries began to be built at parish churches.[3] Many of the fifth- and sixth-century baptisteries extant today in Tunisia were not associated with cathedrals.

By the eighth century in many areas in the West, adult baptism had largely been replaced by infant baptism, partly due to the high infant mortality rate and parental fears resulting from the doctrine of original sin. Fonts no longer needed to be large enough for the submersion or immersion of adults. Thus began a decline in baptismal theology and baptismal practice—and in the size and design of baptismal fonts. In some places existing fonts were made smaller. In other places, new fonts were constructed—but instead of pools which were completely in the ground, fonts with sides partially above the ground were built.

Eventually the norm became pools which were totally above the ground. For a time they retained the visual sense of being pools, and infant submersion and immersion were practised. In at least one, in Cividale, Italy, even adult submersion could still be practised.[4]

However, fonts continued to become smaller and smaller. Rather than looking like pools or basins, they began to resemble tanks and tubs. By the twelfth and thirteenth centuries they were set on bases or one or more pedestals. In the

---

[1] See chapter 3 for description.
[2] See Fisher and Stevick.
[3] Regarding the situation in North Africa, see Duval (1989).
[4] See chapter 3.

Romanesque and Gothic periods in Europe, these fonts could still accommodate infant immersion (and often, infant submersion). Most fonts during this time were sculpted stone[1], but some were wood, and in England there were numerous decorated lead tubs (which were most frequently round).[2]

As affusion (pouring) replaced immersion and submersion by the late sixteenth century, fonts became minimal. In time they resembled birdbaths, then salad bowls, and finally teacups. The rich biblical and patristic understandings of baptism as birth, burial, and bath had been lost. It became impossible to interpret the font as womb or tomb or even as bathtub. One cannot bathe, not to speak of drown, in a fingerbowl.

This minimalism in fonts is one important factor in parishioners' minimal, if not magical, concepts of baptism. Most people in the Church today understand baptism merely as a 'nice' ceremony with gurgling babies, rather than as a consequential event of death and new life. The rich biblical understanding of water and the profound patristic theology of baptism have largely disappeared from the life of the Church. Through the Middle Ages, deteriorating baptismal practices led to trivial fonts, which in turn has had a deleterious effect on the people's understanding of baptism. People *do* learn from what they see; the question is *what* they learn from the fonts which they see in their parish churches.

Two major factors in the late twentieth century have resulted in new attention to the theology of baptism as well as to providing fonts consistent with that theology: (1) Vatican II and the resulting recovery of the adult catechumenate— first in the Roman Catholic Church, and subsequently also in the Anglican and Lutheran Communions, and (2) publication and reception of the World Council of Churches' Faith and Order paper, *Baptism, Eucharist and Ministry*. At last the trend toward minimalism is beginning to reverse. There is growing ecumenical awareness of the profound meaning of baptism and therefore of the symbolism of water, with the result that parishes are recognizing the need for fonts which enable the abundant use of water. Once again, after so many centuries, fonts are being designed and constructed which accommodate the immersion and even submersion of adults as well as infants.

SHAPES
Since the third century, baptismal fonts have been built in various shapes[3] and in many sizes. The shapes of early-Christian fonts included the simple to the complex, and can be considered in five basic categories:
 1. Simple: rectangle, square, circle
 2. Polygonal: hexagon, octagon
 3. Cruciform: cross, quadrilobe
 4. Polylobe: with six, eight, or twelve lobes
 5. Other

---

[1] See Nordström.
[2] See Bond, chapter VII; and Wall, pp.276-284.
[3] An interesting and helpful, albeit incomplete and sometimes erroneous, typological classification of fonts by shape is provided in Khatchatrian (1982), pp.69-78.

Each of these shapes itself can be simple, or altered in some way. For examples: concave sides might appear on a square or a hexagon; a cross shape might have squared or rounded 'arms'; quadrilobe fonts have lobes of varying lengths. In addition, two shapes might be combined in a single font. Examples: a font of one form at the rim might have a different form at the bottom; a quadrilobe might be set within a circle; a cross might be inscribed with a circle. Examples of all of these shapes and variations will be given in the following chapter.

Baptisteries as well as fonts reflect a variety of shapes and complexity. In some, the upper level of the building differs from its ground plan. In others, the interior differs in plan from the exterior. Also, in their various shapes[1], some baptisteries had single apses, some had niches of rectangular and/or semicircular shape, some had ambulatories, some had columns with arcades, some had columns supporting *ciboria* (canopies) over the fonts, and so on. When considering the shapes of fonts vis-a-vis the baptisteries in which they were placed, the symbolic possibilities and therefore multivalent understandings of baptism are both rich and complex.

ARCHITECTURAL ANTECEDENTS

Ancient baptisteries and fonts had architectural antecedents in the Roman world.[2] The rectangular font at Dura-Europos resembled both basins in the Roman baths in the same town[3] and Roman (as well as Syrian) tombs.[4]

Some early fonts were built over baths, convenient because both the water source and drain would be in place. Some baptisteries and fonts in the fourth century, including at the Lateran in Rome[5], seem to have been modelled after baths. But why? Was it because of the understanding of baptism as bathing, or was it simply because the baths suggested a practical way to construct a facility for a large volume of water? The rationale of the designers is not known. However, it does seem that Roman public bathing practices influenced to some degree early Christian baptismal practices, and thus it is not surprising that this culture would also have influenced baptismal architecture.[6]

While the first stage of the Lateran baptistery in Rome was influenced by bath architecture[7], the other most important ancient baptistery in the West, in Milan, was influenced instead by burial places, specifically by imperial mausolea—buildings for the burial of members of the imperial family.[8] Once again, however, what is not known is why the baptistery was built on the octagonal plan of a

---

[1] For plans, see Khatchatrian (1962); for a typology of shapes, see Khatchatrian (1982).
[2] See Krautheimer (1969); Krautheimer (1980), p.50; Khatchatrian (1982); Mirabella Roberti (1984); Fete; Swift; and Stauffer, 'Cultural Settings of Architecture for Baptism in the Early Church'.
[3] Kraeling, p.26. See also Krautheimer (1969), p.132.
[4] Hopkins, pp.249ff.
[5] See chapter 3.
[6] Fête.
[7] Fête.
[8] Mirabella Roberti (1984).

nearby mausoleum. Some scholars have been quick to say that it was to give architectural expression to the paschal understanding of baptism, and that therefore using the plan of a burial edifice was only natural. But it is also possible that the octagonal plan was simply a good structural design for both types of centralized space.

CANOPIES AND COVERS

In the early Christian period, fonts were quite often surmounted by a dome-type canopy, commonly termed a *ciborium*, They were free-standing, supported by columns (usually numbering between four and twelve). Some of the *ciboria* may have been decorated with mosaic.

In the late medieval period, many fonts were once again surmounted by canopies, often as a means of giving visual prominence to the font. Unfortunately, the canopies rather than the water in the font became the primary visual symbol of Baptism. Sometimes the canopies were so monumental that the fonts themselves were barely noticeable.

Actual font covers originated in the thirteenth century. The medieval people had begun to steal the consecrated water in fonts to use for witchcraft and black magic. A canon law was enacted requiring locked covers on fonts. Originally the covers were flat, but eventually they were recognized for their decorative possibilities, and they took on monumental shapes of their own.[1]

---

[1] See Bond, part IV.

3. Early Christian Fonts

In the last chapter a brief survey of the history of fonts was given. In the present chapter examples from this history in the West will be described. Primary attention will be given to early Christian fonts (third to eighth centuries) in Italy, France, and Tunisia, with a few also from Switzerland. Some have been excavated and restored, while others need re-excavation.

Where possible, measurements are those taken by the author *in situ*. For fonts in which damage or the need for re-excavation precludes such measurements (especially for depths), dimensions have been drawn from excavation reports or other sources.

The early Christian fonts described here are organized by shape, in two types of semi-chronological order. First, the shapes themselves are presented in approximate chronological order according to when they first appeared; for example, the rectangular shape is the oldest, while the quadrilobe is relatively late. Second, within the sections by shape, the fonts are presented in relative chronological order. It should be noted, however, that it is often not possible to provide precise dates, even by century. In many cases, there is no determinative archaeological evidence for dating, and dates are contested for a number of fonts.

Early Christian fonts which were transformed over the years from one shape into another are included after the section on 'other shapes'. These transformations are often quite interesting, even when they sometimes entailed reducing the size of the font. Several examples: The original rectangular font in Geneva, Switzerland, was soon transformed into an octagonal shape. The early hexagonal font in the church of Servus in Sbeitla, Tunisia, was later made into a smaller quadrilobe. A circular font in Aosta, Italy, was made into a cruciform pool, and then into an octagon.

The symbolism of the various shapes is briefly discussed in each section. However, Richard Krautheimer's caution about over-interpretation should be noted:

'. . . the symbolical significance is something which merely accompanied the particular form which was chosen for the structure. It accompanied it as a more or less uncertain connotation which was only dimly visible and whose specific interpretation was not necessarily agreed upon. Yet as a connotation it was nearly always coupled with the pattern which had been chosen. Its very vagueness explains the variety of interpretations given to one and the same form either by one or by different authors.'[1]

RECTANGULAR FONTS

As already noted, the rectangle is the most ancient font shape; the earliest example is mid-third century. The rectangle was the common shape of ancient sarcophagi and burial niches, and it remains the shape of contemporary coffins

---

[1] Krautheimer (1969), p.122.

in the twentieth century. Rectangular fonts have thus often been interpreted with reference to baptism as burial with Christ (Romans 6.4; Galatians 2.20a; Colossians 3.3).[1]

While the rectangle was the common form for fonts in the third and fourth centuries, most of them have been destroyed over the years. Only a few of the most ancient ones remain.

Dura-Europos, Syria

This mid-third-century font, extremely important because it is the oldest to be found by archaeologists, was in a house church in which one room (also approximately rectangular) had been transformed into a baptistery. The font was installed against the west wall of the room. As noted in the last chapter, this tub-type font with its niche resembled both Roman and Syrian tombs, and the way it was constructed matched that of basins in Roman baths in Dura.[2]

The font was an irregular rectangle measuring 1.63 metres long, with a slightly varying width of approximately 1 metre; it was about .95 metres deep.[3] Faced in white waterproof plaster, it was not connected to a water source, and no drain was found by excavators. Ledges within the font permitted the candidate to sit, bend over, and be baptized by immersion or pouring.[4]

A canopy, supported by two columns and two pilasters, surmounted the font. Painted blue and studded with white stars, the canopy vault resembled the sky; the ceiling of the baptistery was also painted in this manner. The wall above the font contained a painted scene of a shepherd with sheep. Other walls in the baptistery contained paintings of other narrative biblical scenes[5], including the healing of the paralytic, Adam and Eve, the walking on water, a garden scene (perhaps Paradise?), the woman at the well, David and Goliath, and a sequence of resurrection scenes.

San Ponziano Catacomb, Rome, Italy

This third-century catacomb includes, in a low level, what undoubtedly was a baptismal pool, variously dated from the fifth to the eighth centuries. It served a small community outside the walls of Rome.[6]

When it was in use, the pool was somewhat less than 2 metres long and about 1 metre wide, with a depth of about 1 metre.[7] Fed by a spring or an underground stream, the baptistery has been greatly damaged by heavily infiltrating water[8], and can no longer be measured safely.

---

[1] For example, Davies (1962), p.19.
[2] See chapter 2 section on architectural antecedents.
[3] Kraeling, p.26.
[4] Kraeling, pp. 27, 145, and 148.
[5] For details, see Kraeling, pp. 40-88.
[6] Umberto M. Fasola, secretary of the Pontifical Commission on Sacred Archaeology, in personal letter to the author, 27 December 1984. See also P. Testini, *Archeologia Cristiana* (Desclée, Rome), p.190.
[7] Varying dimensions are given in Cote, p.152; and Rogers, p.335.
[8] For drawings of the baptistery prior to flooding damage, see *DACL* (Tome 2, Pt. 1), column 407; Brown, p.46; Bond, p.6; and Cote, frontispiece.

On the upper rear wall of the font was a fresco (now destroyed by the rising water) of a large cross. Over the font was a fresco of the baptism of Christ, showing him in nearly waist-deep water; on the side are an angel and a deer. The latter is presumed to be a reference to the catechumen's thirsting for God, just as 'a deer longs for flowing streams' (Psalm 42.1-2).

Other Rectangular Fonts
Stage 1 of font I in Aquileia, Italy (see Illustration 9, page 42); stage 1 of font I in Geneva, Switzerland; and stage 2 of the Zurzach, Switzerland, font were rectangular; see below in section on 'Fonts Transformed'.

CIRCULAR FONTS
Round fonts, which in the West originated in fourth-century Rome, were more common in the East than the West. In North Africa, there is more archaeological evidence of circular fonts constructed in what is now Algeria than in what is now Tunisia.

There have been various symbolic interpretations of the circle in Christianity[1], but none of these explanations is as straightforward as, for example, the death-resurrection symbolism of the cruciform shape. Circular fonts may simply have derived from circular basins in Roman baths.

Lateran Baptistery, Rome, Italy
The baptistery at the Basilica of St. John Lateran, the cathedral of Rome, has a very complex history.[2] From the first century, the site held a house which was then made into a domestic bathing facility. Eventually a circular room was constructed with a circular pool in the centre. In the early fourth century the Emperor Constantine gave the property to the bishop of Rome, who adapted the circular room into the first baptistery in the city. The form of the baptistery and its earliest circular font/pool is very similar to that of the round *frigidaria* (cold baths) of the Stabian and Forum Baths in nearby Pompeii. The extraordinarily large interior of the earliest baptistery was nearly 19 metres in diameter and about 18 metres high.

The circular baptismal pool was 8.50 metres in diameter, and was sunken about 1 metre into the floor. It probably contained three steps. Based on Roman bathing practice, it is likely to have been filled with water to the second step. Literary evidence (for which there is, unfortunately, neither archaeological proof nor rebuttal) indicates that the pool was covered with silver, and that water was supplied through seven silver stags (said to weigh about 36 kilograms each) and a

---

[1] Including J. G. Davies' interpretation of round fonts as reflecting the womb of rebirth; (1962), pp.21-22. Krautheimer, in contrast, cites ancient authors' interpretation of the circle as a symbol of virtue (Augustine), and of the Church (Candidus); (1969), p.121.

[2] The author is indebted to Joseph N. Fête for his detailed and well-documented summary in 'The Cultural Background of the Roman Ritual of Baptism' (unpublished thesis, Yale University Divinity School, 1981).

gold lamb (about 13 kilograms) which were on the rim. The water source was a nearby aqueduct, and the water may have been heated before pouring into the font.

Later in the fourth century the baptistery was reconstructed as an octagon, but the font remained circular. Under Sixtus III (432-440), eight pillars with an architrave were installed around the font, creating an ambulatory.[1] The architrave carried an inscription reflecting baptism as birth and bath:

'The city, a people to be consecrated,
here springs into being from fruitful seed:
which the Spirit brings forth from impregnated waters.
Be dipped in the sacred stream, O sinner called to purity:
whom the water will receive old, but bring forth new.
There is no distinction among those born again,
whom one font, one Spirit, one faith make one.
From her virginal womb Mother Church gives birth in the stream
      to her children,
whom she conceives through the breath of God.
Wouldst thou be pure, cleanse thyself in this bath,
whether thou art oppressed by original sin or by thine own guilt.
This is the fountain of life, which purges the whole world,
taking its course from the wound of Christ.
Hope for the Kingdom of Heaven, ye who are reborn in this font;
the blessed life does not accept those who are born only once.
Let not the number or the kind of his sins frighten anyone;
born of this stream he will be holy.'[2]

Font I, Orthodox Baptistery, Ravenna, Italy

Dating to the first half of the fifth century, this octagonal baptistery (which some believe to have been constructed over a Roman bath) is one of the most famous extant edifices from the early Christian world, even though the font which is now visible dates only to about the twelfth century. It is also known as the Neonian baptistery, after Bishop Neon (451-475), under whom the decoration was installed. The baptistery and its vast mosaic decoration have received much attention by art historians.[3] The dome was built about fifty years after the baptistery itself; earlier, it probably had a wooden roof.[4] The mosaic in the dome shows the twelve apostles radiating from a scene of the baptism of Christ; the latter was heavily restored in both the fourteenth and nineteenth centuries, and the mode of the baptism may have been altered.

The original floor of the baptistery was three metres below the present floor. The earliest font was internally circular[5], and it measured about 2.7 metres in

---

[1] For a description of the Sistine renovation, see Krautheimer (1980), pp.49-50.
[2] Translation in Underwood, p.55; see also his analysis of the inscription, pp.55-61.
[3] Including Kostof, Van Dael, and Wharton.
[4] See Kostof, p.41; and Krautheimer (1986), p.176.
[5] Kostof, pp.36 and 140; see also Khatchatrian (1962), fig. 339.

diameter.[1] It has been said that this font was built over a bishop's tomb.[2]

The medieval octagonal font which is now visible was built on the foundations of the original circular font.

Mustis, Tunisia *(Illustration 1)*

North-east of the present-day town of El Krib, the Mustis ruins include a Byzantine basilica and baptistery. The essentially quadrilateral baptistery is on the west side of the apse and contains a well-preserved circular font probably from the sixth century.

The in-ground circular font is approximately 1 metre deep and contains two steps. The drain is intact.

Partway up the apse wall, a very short distance from the font, is a large circular stone cistern, which may somehow have supplied water to the font.

Illustration 1 — Mustis.

---

[1] Wharton, p.363.
[2] Kostof, p.6.

Other Circular Fonts
Stage 1 of font I, and stage 2 of font II, both in Aosta, Italy; and stage 2 of font I in Aquileia, Italy, were round; see below in the section on 'Fonts Transformed'.

OCTAGONAL FONTS
Dating to the early fourth century, the eight-sided form is one of the most ancient in the West for fonts as well as for baptisteries. Octagonal fonts were built frequently in Europe (especially in Italy and France), but they are not known in North Africa (nor in the East).

Medieval numerology has given rise to much attention to the symbolism of the number eight, but it received symbolic interpretation also in the early Christian period.[1] The predominant reference is to the Eighth Day, the day of Christ's Resurrection, the eschatological dawning of the new age which is entered in baptism. Thus, baptism is understood as resurrection with and new life in Christ (Romans 6.4b, 9-11; Colossians 3.1).

San Stefano alle Fonti, Milan, Italy
This earliest baptistery in Milan dates to the first third of the fourth century. Its font is the most ancient octagonal font discovered by archaeologists; thus it is effectively the prototype for the numerous octagonal fonts in the West. It may have been where Ambrose was baptized in A.D. 374.[2]

This baptistery was located to the north-east of (but was not attached to) the apse of the Basilica Vetus, also known as the church of Santa Maria Maggiore, over which the present Duomo (cathedral) was later constructed. The font excavation is located below the sacristy of the Duomo, but it is entered from the exterior.

The font is an irregular octagon, measuring approximately 3.70 metres across, with sides between about 1.25 and 1.50 metres long. A water channel and drain are in place. A ledge on at least five of the interior sides of the font may have served as a step (on the other sides, destruction precludes knowing whether there was a ledge).

San Giovanni alle Fonti, Milan, Italy *(Illustration 2)*
Commonly known as the Ambrosian Baptistery, this octagonal baptistery with its octagonal font was probably constructed in A.D. 379-381[3], while Ambrose was bishop.[4] It was located to the south-east of (but was detached from) the apse of the Basilica Nova, also known as the cathedral of Santa Tecla. Most scholars believe this baptistery to be the site of Augustine's baptism by Ambrose at the Easter Vigil, 24 April 387.[5]

---

[1] See Krautheimer (1969), pp.149-150; Dölger, pp.153-187; and Underwood, pp.80-89.

[2] Ambrose was elected bishop, baptized, ordained a presbyter, and consecrated bishop within a two-week period in late 374.

[3] According to its excavator, Mario Mirabella Roberti, in a personal conversation in Milan in 1985. Krautheimer, however, believes that the baptistery was more probably built about A.D. 350, and only decorated by Ambrose; (1986), p.480, footnote 18.

[4] His consecration as bishop of Milan was on 7 December 374.

[5] See Mirabella Roberti and Paredi.

The fourth-century cathedral and baptistery were largely destroyed in the sixteenth century, although parts of the lower baptistery walls and much of the structure of the font remain. The excavation is entered by steps at the rear of the Duomo.

The baptistery was probably modelled after the octagonal imperial mausoleum of Maximian (built in the late third century), within the fortress of San Vittore al Corso in Milan.[1] It is similar to the mausoleum of Sant' Aquilino, attached to the imperial basilica of San Lorenzo.[2] The exterior of the baptistery is 19.30 metres in diameter, and is constructed of brick. The interior was a domed central space with walls of alternating rectangular and semi-circular niches.[3] Eight large columns stood at the perimeter of the room, between the niches. The pavement of the baptistery was a geometric design in black and white marble.[4]

At least some of the interior walls were painted, and there was a gold and polychromatic dome mosaic[5] but unfortunately the design can no longer be determined.

Illustration 2 — San Giovanni, Milan.

---

[1] See Mirabella Roberti (1984); and Mirabell Roberti and Paredi.
[2] Sant' Aquilino itself was also modelled after the mausoleum of Maximian. While the latter is no longer extant, Sant' Aquilino can be seen today and gives a reasonable idea of how the Ambrosian baptistery probably looked.
[3] This baptistery is generally accepted as the first octagonal niched baptistery, and it is believed to have served as the prototype for many similar baptisteries in the fifth century, especially in what are now northern Italy, Provence, and Istria.
[4] For detailed plan, see Mirabella Roberti and Paredi, following p.22.
[5] Some of the tesserae of various colours and shapes are on display adjacent to the baptistery.

The baptistery was entered by a door in one of the rectangular niches, and exited directly opposite.

The in-ground octagonal font is more than 5 metres across, and the eight sides are each about 2.10 metres long. It was about .80 metres deep.[1] There were three steps on seven of the sides; no step existed on the eighth side, where the bishop stood to speak the baptismal formula. The font was completely faced in white Greek marble.

The incoming water pipe and the drain, found in the excavation, are on two contiguous sides. The water was apparently supplied by a cistern. An eight-distich inscription[2], perhaps from around the bottom of the dome, is famous for its emphasis on the octagonal shape of the baptistery and pool, and thus of the primary paschal meaning of baptism:

'This temple of eight niches was built for holy use;
 an octagonal font is worthy of this gift.
It was fitting that on this number
 the hall of holy baptism
 was built, by which true salvation has returned to the people
 in the light of Christ rising again.
For he who was freed from the prison
 of death frees the dead from their tombs,
 frees from every stain of guilt those who confess their sins,
 and washes them in the stream of the purifying font.
May they come quickly to this place.
 Let those who want to discard the faults of a shameful life
 here wash their hearts and bear pure breasts.
Even though in darkness,
 may one dare to approach,
 for one will depart shining whiter than snow.
The holy ones hasten to this place
 because no one just is able to shun the waters.
In these [waters] is the reign and purpose of God,
 and the glory of [God's] justice.
For what is more divine than this,
 that in an instant the sin of a people falls away?'[3]

The understanding of baptism as a combination of burial and resurrection with Christ, and as cleansing from sin and guilt, is reflected also in the baptismal homilies of Ambrose.[4] It is significant also that Ambrose spoke of the font as a grave[5] and a tomb[6]; perhaps he had in mind the imperial mausoleum after which the baptistery was modelled.

---

[1] Mirabella Roberti and Paredi, p.19.

[2] The inscription is now preserved only in a ninth-century codex. The inscription is often attributed to Ambrose, but its authorship is not really known. See Latin text and detailed treatment in Dölger.

[3] The author is indebted to Edward Yarnold and Samuel Torvend for assistance with this translation.

[4] For examples, see *De Sacramentis* I:12, II:20 and 23, III:2; *De Mysteriis* III:11, 14:21.

[5] *De Sacramentis* II:19.

[6] *De Sacramentis* III:1.

Ambrose baptized by triple immersion[1] but it is not known whether he *meant* immersion (in which the body is only partly in the water) or, rather, submersion (in which the entire body is under the water). Whatever method he used, his interpretation was paschal, consonant with the practice of baptizing at the paschal vigil on Easter eve.

While it is known that the *pedilavium* (post-baptismal footwashing) was practised in Milan[2], no archaeological evidence has indicated where it took place.

Lyon, France

The baptistery of St. Stephen, a rectangular building with a small apse, is outside the north wall of the present cathedral. It was heated by a hypocaust.[3]

The octagonal in-ground font[4], preserved and partially reconstructed, dates to the late fourth century and was in use through the eighth.[5] In its original form, the exterior of the font measured 3.66 metres across.[6] Subsequently the interior of the font was reduced in size, but it remained octagonal. It is less than a metre deep. The water channel and drain pipe were found in the excavation. The font was, at least in some of its stages, covered by a *ciborium*, supported by eight columns.

Font II, Geneva, Switzerland

In the fifth century the baptistery[7] in Geneva was doubled in size, its apse greatly enlarged, and a second font was constructed. This new font was to the west of the earlier font, and overlapping it on one side.[8]

A column was placed at each corner of the new in-ground octagonal font, presumably to support an architrave and perhaps a *ciborium*. The font was originally 2.50 metres across. The water was fed through a wood pipe from a deep well some distance away, and drained out the bottom of the font.[9]

In the sixth and seventh centuries the interior of the font was twice reduced in size—first to 1.80 metres across, and then to 1.20 metres across[10]—but the octagonal shape was retained (although in its smallest form it is nearly circular in appearance). The depth of the final stage is almost .50 metres; the depths of the earlier stages are not known.

The first two forms of the font were revetted in white marble. However, the third form was faced with stucco which was not waterproof; therefore it is presumed that immersion was no longer practised in Geneva by the late sixth century.[11]

---

[1] *De Sacramentis* II:20

[2] *De Sacramentis* III:4-7.

[3] Khatchatrian (1982), p.115.

[4] There may have been a more primitive font in Lyon, but no traces remain.

[5] Reynaud (1986), p.101.

[6] Reynaud (1986), p.101; see plans and reconstruction, pp.100, 102-103.

[7] See below, the section on 'Fonts Transformed', for information on font I and its baptistery.

[8] See Bonnet (1986), site plan inside front cover, and pp.24-37.

[9] The pipe, drain, and well are extant and visible in the excavation under the old San Pierre cathedral.

[10] Bonnet (1980), p.183.

[11] See Bonnet (1986), p.36; and (1980), p.183.

Castelseprio, Italy

In the fifth century, a church was constructed in this north-eastern Italian town, with an octagonal apsidal baptistery[1] attached to the north side of the apse of the church. The baptistery is connected to the north aisle of the church via a short corridor.

The small octagonal in-ground font has sides of about .90 metres each; internally it is about 1 metre across. It was less than 1 metre deep.

Just west of the font is a unique circular vessel which has been the subject of many theories. Some have interpreted it as a second font, but it may simply have been a cistern.

Fréjus, France *(Illustration 3)*

Probably early in the fifth century, a baptistery was built here with a plan which was square on the exterior, and octagonal on the interior. The interior included alternating semicircular and rectangular niches (similar in plan on the interior, but not the exterior, to baptistery II in Milan).

The octagonal font is about 1.35 metres across at the top and about .80 metres deep; the circular bottom level is about .90 metres in diameter. It was revetted with marble, and contained one step. A low parapet wall, in octagonal shape and presently about .35 metres high, surrounded the font on seven sides. On the

Illustration 3 — Fréjus.

---

[1] See Mirabella Roberti (1982).

eighth side the parapet opened, apparently to admit the candidates to the water. The angles of the parapet were buttressed with bases and columns which may have supported a *ciborium.*

To the south of the font is a second hole (unique in France) in the baptistery pavement, in which there is a terra cotta bowl measuring 1.20 metres across at the top, .40 metres across at the bottom, and .38 metres deep.[1] Though hypothesized as a vessel for the *pedilavium,* its function is truly unknown.[2]

Aix-en-Provence, France
Located off the rear right aisle of the present Cathedral of St.- Saveur, this fifth-century baptistery is square on the exterior, and effectively octagonal on the interior. Eight columns surrounding the font form an ambulatory.

The octagonal font is about 1.60 metres across and .70 metres deep. No steps remain. An apparent water channel and drain are visible.

Riez, France
This relatively small baptistery is an octagonal space set within a square exterior. It contains four semicircular niches, and there were doors on opposing sides (without niches). Probably dating from the fifth century, the exterior was later badly restored.[3]

The font, now partially destroyed, was 1.25 metres across and .43 metres deep; a water channel was discovered.[4]

Riva San Vitale, Switzerland
Dating to about the year A.D. 500[5], this baptistery is square on the exterior (at ground level) but octagonal with niches on the interior.

The in-ground font is octagonal. In the medieval period, a circular above-ground font was built over the original pool; they are approximately the same diameter.[6] Presumably the first font was used for baptizing adults, and the second for infants.

'Font III,' Geneva, Switzerland
Approximately eight metres to the north-east of font II, another octagonal pool was constructed in the sixth or seventh century, although it appears that font II remained in use. The new pool was located in a new rectangular room adjacent to the new, enlarged apse of the 'north cathedral'. This pool is 2 metres across; its depth is not known. It was built over a well, into which it apparently drained. The purpose of this pool is not known. It has sometimes been termed a font, although its excavator has hypothesized that it might have been used for pre-baptismal bathing.[7]

---

[1] Goettelmann, p.45.
[2] Février (1981), p.29.
[3] The baptistery is now used as a display area for archaeological remains.
[4] David-Roy, p.57.
[5] Krautheimer (1986), p.177.
[6] See photo in Buhler (1986), fig. 7.
[7] Bonnet (1980), p.184.

Varese, Italy
This northern Italian site is unique for having three fonts, all visible, built sequentially on top of each other during a ten-century period.[1] The earliest font, which was octagonal, was built in the ground in the seventh century, and was probably used for adult immersion. Then, in the twelfth or thirteenth century, an above-ground octagonal font was built on the top of the earlier pool, and used for infant immersion or submersion. The exterior sides of this second font are decorated with Romanesque sculpture. Finally, in the Baroque period, in the seventeenth or eighteenth century, a tiny covered single-pedestal font was placed inside the Romanesque font. Only affusion or aspersion would have been possible in this small Baroque font. This one site, therefore, provides a good visual summary of the decline from paleo-Christian baptismal pools to the Baroque minimalism of tiny monopod fonts.

Cividale, Italy *(Illustration 4)*
Now displayed in a room off the south aisle of the Duomo, this octagonal above-ground font was originally in an octagonal baptistery (destroyed in the seventeenth century). Constructed of marble in the eighth century, the font still gives the visual impression of a pool, even though it was not in the ground, and it is

Illustration 4 — Cividale.

---

[1] See photo in Colombo and Garancini, p.7.

reported to have been used for the immersion (and perhaps submersion?[1]) of adults in the eighth century. Eight slender columns are mounted on the rim of the font, supporting a decorated arcade; at one time there was probably a canopy. The eight sides of the font measure about 1.25 metres each. Internally, the font is 1.30 metres across at the bottom, and about 2 metres across at the top. It is approximately 1.20 metres deep. There are two internal steps (or three, if the rim is counted).

Originally there were three external steps on one of the sides, so that an adult could enter the water.

Early Lombard Romanesque reliefs adorn the remaining seven external sides, as well as the arches over the colonnade. Among the figures on the arches are peacocks drinking water and eating grapes, lambs, vines, fish, and deer. On one of the side panels of the font are symbols of the four evangelists.

Other Octagonal Fonts
Stage 2 of font I in Geneva, Switzerland; and stage 3 of font I, and stage 1 of font II in Aosta, Italy, were all octagonal. See below in the section on 'Fonts Transformed'.

HEXAGONAL FONTS
The six-sided form for fonts began to appear in Europe in the fifth century and within the same century also in North Africa. Hexagonal fonts were especially popular in northern Italy and the adjacent Adriatic area, as well as in what is now Tunisia.

The usual interpretation is that the number six is a symbolic reference to the sixth day of the week, Friday, the day on which Christ was crucified and died. Thus, hexagonal fonts would seem to refer to baptism as being united with Christ in his death (Romans 6.3, 5a, 6; Galatians 2.20a; Colossians 3.3). Another interpretation was that the hexagon symbolized the Old Adam, created on the sixth day.[2]

Font II, Aquileia, Italy
The very important paleo-Christian site[3] in this north-eastern Italian town is extremely complex. The baptistery located to the west of the present church is undergoing further excavation at the time of writing, and conclusions on the three fonts which are 'stacked' on top of each other in the baptistery must await publication of this further work by archaeologists. However, it appears that the baptistery, probably from the fifth century, is an octagon (with four semi-circular niches) on the interior, in an exterior which is square at the lower level and octagonal at the upper. The fonts were hexagonal. (Regarding the hexagonal-octagonal symbolism, see below, on nearby Grado.)

---

[1] See Rogers, p.347.
[2] Krautheimer (1969), p.148, footnote 164.
[3] See Mirabella Roberti (1978).

Grado, Italy

The octagonal baptistery[1] which presently stands detached from the north side of the apse of the Duomo (S. Euphemia) was constructed in the sixth century, probably over the ruins of an earlier square baptistery. The present structure, which is well-preserved, has a projecting apse on one side, opposite the entrance.

The original pavement and font were below the present floor, as is also the case at Ravenna. The original in-ground font, like the present medieval above-ground replacement, was hexagonal.

Much attention has been given to the combination of hexagonal fonts in octagonal baptisteries, such as in Aquileia (II), Grado, and Lomello.[2] Usually the interpretation of the hexagonal-octagonal combination is paschal.[3]

Cimiez, France

Now a section of Nice, Cimiez is an ancient Greco-Roman site (Cemenelum) which included three bath complexes. The Western bath was destroyed in the late fourth century, and in the fifth century a cathedral and baptistery were built within its remains. The nearly rectangular baptistery was built over the furnaces, adjacent to the north side of the cathedral nave. Eight columns formed an ambulatory in the baptistery, and the font itself was surrounded by six more columns which supported a *ciborium*.[4]

The in-ground font is hexagonal at the top level, and rectangular within the lower level. The hexagon is about 1.60 metres across and about .85 metres deep. There are two steps within the hexagonal level, and two more down into the rectangular level. A channel leading into the top of the font *may* have provided water, but no drain has been found.

San Marcello, Rome, Italy

This font, which can now be viewed through a plexiglass dome from the lobby of the Banco di Roma which is adjacent to San Marcello Church, is from the fifth century. It is an irregular hexagon, with six small lobes radiating outward. It has two steps on three adjacent sides. Revetted in white marble, the interior of the font is 2.50 metres across.

---

[1] See Zovatto (1947-1948) and (1971).

[2] The same combination existed in Tabarka, Tunisia, and in Porec (Parenzo), on the Istrian peninsula of the former Yugoslavia.

[3] For example, Davies wrote 'As he entered the octagonal building, the catechumen was buoyed with hope in the Resurrection of Christ; as he entered the hexagonal font, he knew he was to die with Christ, but as he left the font and stood once more in the eight-sided room he also knew that he was to walk in newness of life' (1962), p.21. While this interpretation is certainly logical, it is not known if this (or any, for that matter) symbolism was intentional on the part of those who designed fonts and baptisteries—or whether it was in the minds of catechumens and neophytes, or of those who presided.

[4] Benoît, pp.146-7.

Colour Plate 1 — Kélibia.

VITALIS
ET CARDE
LAVO IV
MISA

Colour Plate 2
Vitalis, Sbeitla.

Colour Plate 3 — Guardian Angel, London.

Colour Plate 4 — Redeemer, Chimacum, WA.

Dermech I, Carthage, Tunisia (*Illustration 5*)

The nearly square peristyle baptistery of this basilical complex[1] is attached to the far wall of the north aisle of the church, and there were two or three doors between the church and the baptistery. The baptistery dates to the fifth or sixth century.[2] The peristyle of the baptistery, formed by twelve columns, created an ambulatory. Four additional columns probably supported a *ciborium* over the font. The baptistery's pavement was mosaic: large panels intricately decorated with geometric shapes (including many octagons), flowers, and birds.[3]

Illustration 5 — Dermech I, Carthage.

---

[1] The church complex known as Dermech I is quite close to the ruins of the huge Antonine Baths, which sit on the Mediterranean shore of Carthage (now a suburb of Tunis). The name 'Dermech' is a corruption of *thermae*, the Latin word for 'baths.' The entire site (including baths, basilicas, and what probably were houses) is now a national archaeological park.

[2] A small longitudinal chapel (perhaps a consignatorium?) is attached to the east side of the baptistery. Its date is unknown.

[3] Only a small portion of the mosaic remains *in situ*, and it is badly worn. However, a small panel from the pavement was installed in the Bardo Museum in Tunis, and, interestingly, it includes what appears to be a chalice framed by an octagon.

The font has always been described and depicted as a hexagon. It does, indeed, have a significant hexagonal form near the top. However, the hexagon is one level down from the baptistery pavement; at the level of the pavement, what appears to be the orifice of the font is an irregular circle.[1] There are two steps each on the north-east and south-east sides.[2] The font is about 1 metre deep. At the 'top' hexagonal level, it measures 1.50 metres across; the bottom of the pool, which was circular, is .70 metres in diameter. The hexagonal sides average .80 metres long. The font was revetted in white marble, some of which is still intact.

Water from the font drained below ground into a cistern which is about metres away; the head of the cistern is at ground level in the north ambulatory of the baptistery. Although the original excavator reported also a water source[3], it has not been found in more recent exploration.

Damous el-Karita, Carthage, Tunisia
This site, located outside the old walls of the city of Carthage, includes one of the largest churches (a nave plus eight aisles) of ancient Tunisia. Unfortunately, confusing ancient overbuilding, as well as prior destructive excavation and, now, thick growth all make the site difficult to understand and to explore. Its date is uncertain, but perhaps fifth century.

For such a huge church, the hexagonal font is relatively small. It measures approximately 2.50 metres across, with sides averaging .90 metres long. There are three steps on two non-parallel sides (as at Dermech I). The font is too filled-in to determine its depth.

Lomello, Italy
Variously dated from the fifth to seventh centuries, this baptistery is octagonal with eight small niches (alternating rectangular and semicircular) radiating out.

The hexagonal font has been altered at various times. On the interior is a small semi-circular projection from which, according to Davies, the presbyter could stand to preside at baptisms.[4]

Other Hexagonal Fonts
Stage 1 of the font in the church of Servus in Sbeitla, Tunisia, was hexagonal. See below, the section on 'Fonts Transformed'.

---

[1] It is a puzzle as to why this shape has not appeared on *any* plans. Further archaeological work is required before conclusions about it can be drawn. It is, thus, not technically possible at present to determine the shape of the font; following tradition it is here classified as hexagonal.

[2] Why the steps were not placed on two opposite (that is, parallel) sides is also a mystery, especially since here that would have put them on an east-west axis.

[3] Gauckler, p.15; see also Vaultrin, p.112.

[4] Davies (1962), p.69.

SQUARE FONTS

Relatively few square fonts have been found, especially in the West. In North Africa, there are ruins of several in what is now Algeria, but only two are presently known in Tunisia. In Europe, several have been found in the former Yugoslavia, and one each in Switzerland and Germany, but none in either France or Italy.

Font I, Uppenna, Tunisia

The architectural site of Uppenna (also known as Henchir Fraga or Henchir Chigarnia) is north of the present-day town of Enfidaville, on Tunisia's east coast.

The first church which stood on the site, built in the late fourth or early fifth century, included a rectangular baptistery with a square in-ground font[1] approximately 1.40 metres across. It had two steps on each side and was over 1 metre deep. There appears to be a drain at the bottom of one side.

Maktar, Tunisia *(Illustration 6)*

The basilica of Hildeguns (the name comes from a tomb found at the entrance to the church), one of several churches in this once-flourishing town, was probably a cathedral.[2] It was destroyed and rebuilt twice, and in its third form included a baptistery. It probably dates to the sixth century.

Illustration 6 — Maktar.

---

[1] See photos and plans in Duval (1973), Tome II, pp.88-94.
[2] Duval (1973), Tome II, p.139.

The church is on an east-west axis, and the baptistery is within the walls of the church, behind the apse.[1] The square baptistery, about 3.70 metres across, itself has a small apse at its east end.

The font was built over a cistern. It was covered by a ciborium mounted on four columns. The font measures 1.80 x 1.80 metres and has a step on three of the sides; the fourth (eastern) side does not have a step. It was covered with mosaic (which seemed to imitate water), much of which is now gone. The bottom of the font is also destroyed, but the depth was 1.24 metres.[2]

Other Square Fonts

Stage 1 of the font in Zurzach, Switzerland, was square; see below in the section on 'Fonts Transformed'.

CRUCIFORM FONTS

Cross-shaped fonts have an obvious and immediate visual reference to the crucifixion and resurrection of Jesus Christ (Romans 6.3-11). The meaning is bivalent: both death and victory over death, the sixth day and the eighth day combined.

Cruciform fonts first appeared in the West in the fifth or sixth century. They were particularly popular in North Africa (as well as in the East).

Thuburbo Majus, Tunisia *(Illustration 7)*

In about the fifth century, the southern half of a large pagan temple from the second or third century was transformed into a Christian church.[3] The baptistery was placed in the cella (the room in which the statue of the divinity had been displayed) of the former temple. The cella/baptistery is nearly square, measuring approximately 6 metres per side. Two doors on the south side give access to/from a columned hall (narthex), and one door (in the baptistery's east wall) connects the baptistery with the north aisle of the small church. The mosaic pavement of the baptistery is no longer intact.

The cruciform font, with a circle inscribed at the centre of the top level, measures about 2.60 metres (north-south) by 1.93 metres (east-west). The squared arms of the cross are about .50 metres wide, and each had three steps.[4] The depth of the font cannot be determined without re-excavation, but it was more than 1.10 metres. There is no indication of the water source or drain.

---

[1] The arrangement is thus similar to that of the church of Vitalis in Sbeitla; see below under 'Fonts of other shapes'.

[2] Duval (1973), Tome II, p.139.

[3] For comparative plans of the temple and church, see Lézine (1968), figure 6. For a large detailed plan of the church and baptistery, see Ben Abed-Ben Khader, *et al.*, *Thuburbo Majus*, Vol. II, Fascicle 2 of Margaret A. Alexander and Mongi Ennaifer, *Corpus des Mosaiques de Tunisie* (Tunis: Institut National d'Archéologie et d'Art, 1985), plan 11; photo 188 in the same volume shows a fragment of the baptistery pavement mosaic.

[4] The bottom steps on the northern and southern arms were concave.

It appears from notches in the northern and southern arms that, at a later stage, slabs were inserted across those arms, effectively making the font into a 1.93 x .75 metre rectangle.[1] The hypothesized slabs are not extant.

Illustration 7 — Thuburbo Majus.

Bulla Regia, Tunisia

The sixth-century font in this double-apsed basilica[2] is in the first bay of the nave, just in front of the west apse. The pavement around the font is *opus sectile*. The font was surmounted by a *ciborium*, supported by four columns.

The cruciform font measures 2.16 x 2.76 metres, and it is quite deep: 1.45 metres. The squared arms of the cross are about .61 metres wide. There are four sets of four steps each.

At some point the font was made smaller[3] by inserting marble slabs across two of the arms of the cross, so that only the resulting rectangle needed to be filled with water. Among the hypothesized reasons are that there was a water shortage, or that it was done to enable infant baptism more easily.

---

[1] Such slabs are still in place in the cruciform font at Bulla Regia; see below. The Bulla font in its rectangular stage was slightly longer and deeper.

[2] For an extensive description and analysis of dual-apsed churches in Tunisia, see Duval, *Les églises africaines à deux absides*, two volumes. The books include many photographs and plans of fonts in the churches he covers, including a plan of the Bulla Regia churches and font (Tome II, page 42).

[3] See Duval (1973), Tome II, p.46.

'Carthagenna' Baptistery, Carthage, Tunisia

This site[1] has a large double-apsed church and very large baptistery from the mid-sixth century. The baptistery measures about 14 metres per side. Its external plan is square, but it is effectively octagonal on the interior, with four radiating niches or alveoles which were probably covered by semidomes.[2] The floors of these niches each contained a very large multicolored mosaic scallop shell; the remains of one can still be seen. An octagonal *ciborium* supported by eight pillars surmounted the font. The cruciform font, now partially destroyed, measures about 2.90 metres across, with a centre section about 1.40 metres in diameter. The extant arms of the cross average about .75 metres wide. The font was about 1 metre deep, and was revetted in white marble. (It was, thus, larger but shallower than the cruciform font at Bulla Regia.) There were two opposing flights of steps which, according to the excavator, permitted adults to descend for 'total immersion'.[3] There are cisterns below the baptistery, so it is likely that there was a drain from the font and probably also a water source for it.

El Kantara, Tunisia *(Illustration 8)*

The cruciform El Kantara[4] font is also from the sixth century. It was constructed of re-used[5] slabs of white marble. The arms of the cross are rounded, unlike those at Thuburbo Majus, Bulla Regia, and Carthage. The width of the arms is about .43 metres, and the interior of the pool is about 2.20 metres each direction. There are two steps on each of the four sides. At present the font is only about .50 metres deep.

Font I, Acholla, Tunisia

Another cruciform font with rounded arms is at Acholla (known today as Bou Tria). Regrettably, it is now badly damaged, and two of the arms of the cross are completely destroyed. Based on what is remaining, the font appears to have been about 1.40 metres across. There were steps on two sides. The depth can no longer be determined.[6] The cross-shaped pool seems to have been set within a circular form.[7]

---

[1] It is familiarly referred to as the 'Michigan baptistery' because it was excavated by a University of Michigan team under the direction of John Humphrey, or the *'super-marché* site' because it is adjacent to the supermarket in Carthage. However, it has been called 'Carthagenna' by Liliane Ennabli (who excavated the church) in her article 'La Basilique de Carthagenna'. The site has a fine small early-Christian museum which includes an exhibit of the method of tubular vaulting which was used in the baptistery.

[2] Humphrey, p.167.

[3] Humphrey, p.167. 'Total immersion' is the same mode as submersion.

[4] It is also known as the Meninx font, which is how it is labelled at the Bardo Museum in Tunis, where it is now displayed. It comes from the Tunisian island of Djerba. In Khatchatrian (1962), it is referred to as Henchir Bour Medes. See also *DACL*, Tome 11, Part 1, column 417.

[5] This re-utilization may account for the bizarre holes and channels in some of the slabs.

[6] When examined in 1992, it could be measured down only .43 metres from the rim.

[7] See figs. 2 and 3 in Duval (1980).

Illustration 8 — El Kantara.

La Skhira, Tunisia

This sixth-century rectangular baptistery is attached to another rectangular room behind the west apse of the church.[1] The baptistery pavement was decorated with mosaic, part of which is intact.

The small cruciform pool has rounded arms which are quite irregular in size. Overall, the pool measures about 1.60 metres x 1.90 metres, and it is set within an octagonal form.[2] There were two steps, and the depth of the font was 1.30 metres.[3] The font is now quite filled in, and there has been considerable damage to the octagonal form. No water source or drain was found. The font was surmounted by a *ciborium* supported by four columns.

Other Cruciform Fonts

Stage 2 of font I in Aosta, Italy, was cruciform. See below, the section on 'Fonts Transformed.'

---

[1] See plan in Duval (1973), Tome II, p.255
[2] Photographs of the then-newly excavated font (with its steps) within the octagon are provided by Fendri, plates XVIII and XIX.
[3] Fendri, p.44.

QUADRILOBE FONTS

This four-lobed shape developed out of the cruciform shape[1], of which it is a variation. Thus the meaning is the same, referring to the death and resurrection of Christ. It is also known as quatrefoil and, in French, as *tétraconque*. Quadrilobe fonts were common in Tunisia as well as in Israel.

Kélibia, Tunisia *(Colour Plate 1)*

This late sixth-century quadrilobe font[2] and its surrounding pavement, all covered in mosaic decoration, is the most stunning early-Christian discovery in Tunisia. Originally in a baptistery attached to the south of the apse of the church of Felix in Kélibia (ancient Clupea) on the Cap Bon peninsula of north-eastern Tunisia, it is now reinstalled in the Bardo Museum in Tunis.[3]

The font is set within a raised, irregular circle, in the middle of a square mosaic floor which is 3.10 metres across. The font itself is 2.10 metres across, and slightly more than 1 metre deep. Ledges within the four lobes served as steps; effectively, there were two steps on each side. No water source or drain was found.[4]

In its quadrilobe shape, this font reflects the paschal meaning of Baptism, but its mosaic iconography suggests Baptism as proleptic entry into the abundant life of Paradise.

On the bottom of the pool, and in six other places, are monogrammatic crosses flanked by *alpha* and *omega*, emblematic of Christ and eternal life. On the vertical walls, at mid-level, are fruit trees (apple, olive, fig, and palm) which seem to grow out of the water. On and above the four lobes are fish and dolphins.[5] In Christian iconography of this period and area, fish often represented the baptized, born in the waters of the font. The dolphin was a frequent symbol of the resurrected Christ. One is reminded of what Tertullian had said about baptism: 'We, being little fishes, as Jesus Christ is our great fish, begin our life in the water, and only while we abide in the water are we safe and sound.'[6]

The interior corners of the lobes, at the top register, bear lighted candles, perhaps an iconographic reference to baptism as illumination or enlightenment[7], or maybe symbolic of the Paschal candle. On the upper vertical surfaces

---

[1] Davies (1962), p.22.

[2] See Courtois.

[3] See Yacoub (1978), pp.213-220.

[4] Courtois, p.106.

[5] On the ledge or step of the east lobe is a mosaic figure which has been the subject of much debate. At first glance it looks like a bee, but several scholars believe it to be a *seiche*, or cuttlefish (a mollusc), because it is identical to those shown in many marine mosaics of the same area. Those supporting the honey-bee theory point to the reference to the bee in the *Exultet* of the Easter Vigil. For a summary of the debate, see Palazzo. For additional descriptions and analysis of the mosaic, see the bibliography herein for complete citations for Courtois, Cintas and Duval, Février and Poinssot, Février's later opinion (RAC, 1984), and Alexander (1983).

[6] *De Baptismo* I; translation in Ernest Evans (ed.), *Tertullian's Homily on Baptism* (SPCK, London, 1964) pp.4-5.

[7] Ephesians 1.18; Hebrews 6.4 and 10.32; Justin Martyr, *First Apology* 61.

of the four lobes are mosaic depictions of a dove with an olive branch, Noah's ark between two birds, a chalice, and a cross under a canopy supported by two columns.

The top of the circular rim has an inscription regarding the donor and in honour of Cyprian, bishop of Carthage three centuries earlier.

The four corners of the square pavement mosaic around the font depict four canthari or vases of water, probably a symbol of the font as the fountain of life, or perhaps symbolizing the four rivers of Paradise (Genesis 2.10). Seeming to grow out of the vases are grape vines, perhaps a reference to the eucharist as the culmination of what is begun in the waters of the font.

Jbel Oust, Tunisia

An entirely different type of quadrilobe font was in Jbel Oust. It is essentially a rectangular pool to which, on each side, are attached steps which are rounded at the top level. It dates to the sixth century.

The baptistery here was constructed in the cella of a pagan temple.[1] The baptistery opened onto the court of the temple; the church was built off the court-yard on an adjacent side. Thus the baptistery and church were at a 90-degree angle, and were not directly attached to each other.

The font sat directly over a spring of sulfurous water. (The site was and still is a thermal establishment.)

Overall the font measures about 2.10 metres by 1.65 metres; its rectangular pool is approximately .53 by .90 metres. There are three steps each on two opposite sides. The depth of the pool is unknown, but it was at least .80 metres.

Other Quadrilobe Fonts

Stage 2 of the font in the church of Servus in Sbeitla, Tunisia, was quadrilobe. See below, the section on 'Fonts Transformed.

POLYLOBE FONTS

This form of font is essentially circular, with a varying number of small project-ing lobes or alveoli. In Tunisia the number of lobes is usually eight, but six and twelve are not unknown in North Africa. As a rule they are dated to the sixth century.

Polylobe fonts are one of the mysteries of early Christian architecture in North Africa. They are probably unrelated to quadrilobe fonts, being more likely to carry number symbolism.[2]

Font II, Uppenna, Tunisia

Probably dating from the late sixth century (thus built perhaps two centuries later than the lower, square font on this site), this font is circular at the centre, with eight irregular lobes, set within a square structure.[3] Now quite damaged as

---

[1] See Duval, 'Eglise et temple en Afrique du Nord', pp.290-292.
[2] Duval (1980), p.342; see this entire article for various explanations of polylobe fonts.
[3] For plans and photo, see Duval (1973), Tome II, pp.88-91.

well as overgrown, its depth is impossible to determine. Overall, the pool measures about 1.75 metres across; the interior circle is only .75 metres in diameter.

A few white mosaic *tesserae* remain on one exterior surface. A drain is visible on the exterior of its bottom north side.

Font II, Acholla, Tunisia
Also in poor condition, this in-ground eight-lobed font is set within an irregular circle. The pool measures about 2.10 metres across; the interior round section is 1.30 metres in diameter. The lobes themselves average about .34 metres wide and about the same length. Now completely filled in, its depth is impossible to measure. However, the lobes themselves were reported in 1980 to be an extraordinary .46 metres deep.[1]

Hergla, Tunisia
The square sixth-century baptistery is behind ruins of the apse of a church on a hill facing the sea, between Hammamet and Sousse. The eight-lobed font measures about 2.55 metres across. Several of the lobes are destroyed, but those that remain average about .60 metres across and .50 metres long. The depth of the font is now impossible to determine.

OTHER-SHAPED FONTS
Jucundus, Sbeitla, Tunisia
In Sbeitla (ancient Sufetula), Tunisia, are two fonts of a shape which cannot be described simply.[2] The shape is apparently unique to Sbeitla. Essentially the fonts are rectangles, with bulging exterior sides, and steps on each end. Thus the form is elongated, enabling the neophyte to have a definite sense of passage through the waters, as well as, with the several steps on opposite ends, a clear experience of descent and ascent.

The Chapel of Jucundus (named for a local bishop), which served as the baptistery[3], was attached to the north of the Church of Bellator, which no doubt was the first cathedral of Sbeitla. The church dates to the fourth century, the baptistery in its present excavated form probably to the fifth. The baptistery was rectangular and included a peristyle.

The font, now quite damaged, was oriented roughly north-south, had three steps at each end, and appears to have been covered on the interior with white mosaic (some of which remains). Overall, its interior measures approximately

---

[1] Duval (1980), p.331; see also figs. 4 and 5.
[2] Thus, Duval's description of the Jucundus font: 'Si on ne tient pas compte des escaliers elle est *grosso modo* cruciforme, mais dans la branche de la croix qui fait face à l'abside est inscrit un demi-cylindre verticale; tandis que la branche symétrique était coupée à 46 cm de hauteur par une banquette qui supportait un demi-cylindre montant jusqu'au sommet.' (1971), Tome I, p.120.
[3] See text, plans, and photos in Duval (1971), Tome I, pp.106-133, 296- 297, and plans III and IV at the end of the volume; and Duval and Baratte, pp.44-48.

2.90 metres long. The rectangular bottom of the pool measures about 1.45 metres long and .95 metres wide (not including the concave alveoles). It is about 1 metre deep. At approximately mid-level on one side, there is a ledge (see below, about the Vitalis font ledge).

At a later time, after the new Church of Vitalis was built (see below), a column was set in the font, to hold a reliquary for Jucundus, and as a base for an altar.[1]

Vitalis, Sbeitla, Tunisia *(Colour Plate 2)*

The Church of Vitalis was constructed in the late fifth or early sixth century to the west of the earlier cathedral and baptistery. This new cathedral was approximately double the size of the earlier one.

The baptistery, placed behind the apse, was rectangular with its own small apse.[2] The new font was nearly the same shape as the earlier one (Jucundus), but oriented approximately east-west. It was richly decorated in mosaic. Four column bases were built into the rim, no doubt to support a *ciborium*. Along the north side (just as in the Jucundus font) is a ledge about .60 metres from the bottom; its purpose was apparently simply to take up bulk, reducing the quantity of water necessary in the font.

Counting the rim as a top step, there are four steps on each end. The overall interior of the pool measures about 2.95 metres long and 1.10 metres wide. Its rectangular bottom is 1.25 metres long. The depth of the font is 1.16 metres. There is no evidence of the water source or drain. However, a small orifice is visible on the south wall of the font, about 8 centimetres from the bottom; its purpose is not known.

The mosaic decoration of this font is extraordinary, even given its considerable restoration. The background colour is ecru. The top of the rim contains a dedicatory inscription on the north 'bulge', and a laurel garland around the remainder. Laurel garlands are traditionally understood as symbolic of eternity. In between the sections of garland are rose branches. On both interior sides there is a black Greek cross, perhaps an iconographic reference to baptism as crucifixion and resurrection with Christ. Below the cross on the north side are stylized rosebuds, the flower of Paradise. On the bottom surface of the pool is a monogrammatic cross.

Chateauneuf-de-Grasse, France

Approximately 1.5 kilometres south of this village is Notre-Dame du Brusc, where there are the remains of an irregular seven-sided in-ground font from the sixth or seventh century.[3] It is 1.00 metre across, and about .70 metres deep. There are steps extending out from two opposing sides.

---

[1] See Duval (1971), Tome I, pp.117-119, and 123.
[2] See Duval (1971), Tome I, pp.149, 278-297, and plan V at the end of the volume; and Duval and Baratte, pp.49-58.
[3] See Khatchatrian (1982), p.110.

FONTS TRANSFORMED

It was not uncommon in the ancient world for fonts to be 'remodelled' for a variety of reasons. Sometimes it was done to make the font smaller for easier use with infants. Other times it would seem simply to change the shape.

Font I, Aquileia, Italy *(Illustration 9)*

The sunken rectangular font which is now in the crypt of the extant eleventh-century church may originally have been a bathtub in the Roman house which stood on the site.[1] If so, this domestic bathtub would have served as the font in the *domus ecclesiae* (house church) which preceded the twin basilicas. When, in the second decade of the fourth century, the two parallel basilicas were constructed[2], the original rectangular font was made round and was incorporated into a hexagonal parapet (low wall) located in a transverse structure connecting the two basilicas. A hypocaust may have heated the baptistery and adjacent areas.

In form, although not in placement, this first font in Aquileia is similar to the font at Dura-Europos.[3] The rectangular Aquileia font is 1.73 metres long, .84 metres wide, and .94 metres deep (comparable to that at Dura-Europos); there is one step at each end.

Illustration 9 — Aquileia I.

[1] Kraeling, p.147; and Corbett, p.106 and fig. 1.
[2] Krautheimer (1986), p.43.
[3] Kraeling, p.147.

Font I, Aosta, Italy

The first baptistery at the cathedral in this north-west Italian town was located at the rear of the nave. The baptistery was rectangular.

The first font was originally built in the fourth or fifth century. Its shape can no longer be determined, because of several later transformations, but it was probably polygonal or round; its interior was at least 2.40 metres in diameter.[1]

At a later point in the fifth century, it was made into the unique shape of a cross *patée*; the four arms of the cross angled outward.[2] In this shape, it measured nearly 2 metres across, and had two steps. The bottom of the centre section was octagonal, approximately 1 metre across.

In the sixth century the font was remodelled into an octagon with two steps on every side; the dimensions remained the same. It is in this form that the font appears today, currently measuring approximately .75 metres deep.

Font I, Geneva, Switzerland

While the earliest baptistery in this cathedral complex dated to the mid-fourth century, nothing is known of its font. In about A.D. 400, a second baptistery was constructed, adjacent to the first. It was nearly rectangular and had a small, shallow apse.

The in-ground font was octagonal on the exterior, but rectangular on the interior.[3] It was revetted with marble. Eight columns surrounded the font, no doubt supporting a *ciborium*.

Servus, Sbeitla, Tunisia

The church of Servus[4] may have been the Donatist cathedral in Sbeitla. Its square baptistery, to the north side of the nave, was located in the cella of the temple which existed on the site.

In its earliest, fifth-century, stage, the font[5] was an in-ground hexagon approximately 1.75 metres across. Projecting from two of the sides were sets of two steps each. Four columns surrounded the font, probably supporting a *ciborium*.

In the sixth century, a small quadrilobe font was installed inside the earlier hexagonal font. The quadrilobe measures 1.19 metres across, and is .53 metres deep. Both stages of this font can be seen, although very poor restoration has made the original hexagon appear nearly round.

Font II, Aosta, Italy

In the fifth century a square baptistery[6] was constructed off the north side of the nave of the cathedral. Apparently the earlier baptistery remained in use as well.

---

[1] Bonnet and Perinetti, p.24.
[2] See Bonnet (1989), pp.1418-1421.
[3] See Bonnet (1986), p.25, fig. 3.
[4] See Duval and Baratte, pp.75-78; and Duval, 'Eglise et temple en Afrique du Nord'.
[5] See plan in Duval (1988), p.91.
[6] See Bonnet and Perinetti, pp.28-30.

The font in its first stage was octagonal. In the sixth century it was made into a somewhat smaller circular font, about 1.25 metres across. The water source and drain have been discovered.

Zurzach, Switzerland

In the Kirchlibuck area, to the side of the ruins of a fifth-century church, are the remains of its font. Originally about 1.10 metres square, at some point the font was transformed into a rectangle measuring .90 metres by .50 metres, with a depth of .56 metres.[1] Unfortunately, the font is now completely covered by opaque plastic and cannot be seen.[2]

CONCLUSION

The fourth, fifth and sixth centuries in southern Europe and in North Africa saw the construction of hundreds of fonts which in size, shape, and decoration gave witness to the many meanings of baptism. They were, literally, constructed theology. Not only do they provide significant evidence for church history, but, perhaps even more importantly, they give models for baptismal renewal in today's church. Both patristic texts and early Christian fonts can be used today to help restore baptism to its central place in Christian life and worship. Knowledge about these ancient fonts is thus crucial for pastors and catechists, liturgiologists and theologians, and church architects and liturgical designers.

---

[1] Khatchatrian (1982), p.121; and Buhler (1984), pp.14-15.
[2] See photo in Buhler (1986), fig. 6; and Buhler (1984), p.14.

4. Fonts for Today

The water of the baptismal font is the water of primeval chaos, the mighty water of the Flood, the deadly water of the Red Sea, and the salvific water of the River Jordan. It is the pure water of divine cleansing, the deep water of death, and the river of the water of life. By the grace of God, it is the water that drowns and, at the same time, the water that gives birth. An important task of liturgical renewal today is the provision of fonts which can help make these many meanings of baptism unambiguously evident.

PRINCIPLES
Four principles serve as the basis for considering the design of fonts for the future:
1. A font serves two functions—the symbolic and the ritual.
2. While baptism is certainly multivalent, its chief meaning is paschal—sharing in the death, burial, and resurrection of Christ.
3. Submersion is a fuller ritual enactment of baptism's meanings than any other mode.
4. Fonts are for the baptism of adults as well as infants.

First, a font serves two functions—the symbolic and the ritual

The ritual function of a font is the most obvious: it holds the water needed for baptism. It is a container for the earthly element of the primal sacrament, a vessel for a liturgical action.

But a font is also a symbol of that sacrament, a visual reminder of the fact that we are baptized. It reminds the faithful of their identity: sinners who in the waters of baptism are forgiven; children of God who are the body of Christ in the world; and 'little fish' who in the water are given life in Christ, the great Fish.[1] In baptism we are all 'water babies', just as in the eucharist we are blood brothers and sisters. In baptism we are one in the water, and one with and in Jesus Christ. We are all baptized into one body[2], the one communion of saints.

Baptism is the most important, the most radical, and the most consequential event in human life. The water of the font is not only where this event happens—it is also a visual reminder that it has happened. It is both the *locus* of sacramental action and the symbolic reminder of that action and its meanings.

The font should enable the profound meanings of baptism to be enacted ritually. Likewise, its size, shape, location, and iconography should give the font symbolic intensity and evocative richness.

---

[1] The fish imagery is that of Tertullian; see his *De Baptismo* I (and chapter 1 of this book).

[2] Anglican theologian Paul Avis develops this as 'the baptismal paradigm' for ecclesiology and ecumenism in his book *Christians in Communion* (Liturgical Press, Collegeville, Minnesota, 1990).

Second, while baptism is certainly multivalent, its chief meaning is paschal—sharing in the death, burial, and resurrection of Christ.
Baptism, of course, has many layers of meaning, including washing, incorporation, initiation, enlightenment, birth, death, burial, and resurrection. Perhaps it is because when we think of water in everyday life, we think most often of bathing, that we see washing as the most obvious meaning of baptism. However, New Testament scholar C. F. D. Moule has written that:

> 'in fact Baptism is so much more drastic than this and so much more far-reaching in its consequences, that the New Testament only seldom uses this metaphor. Baptism is essentially *death* and *burial*—not mere *washing*.'[1]

Another New Testament scholar, Oscar Cullmann, concurs; he wrote that 'The temporal centre of all history, the death and resurrection of Christ, is also the centre of the history of Baptism.'[2]

In the sixteenth century, Martin Luther had also emphasized the paschal meaning of baptism:

> 'It is . . . indeed correct to say that baptism is a washing away of sins, but the expression is too mild and weak to bring out the full significance of baptism, which is rather a symbol of death and resurrection . . . The sinner does not so much need to be washed as he needs to die, in order to be wholly renewed and made another creature, and to be conformed to the death and resurrection of Christ, with whom he dies and rises again through baptism . . . It is far more forceful to say that baptism signifies that we die in every way and rise to eternal life, than to say that it signifies merely that we are washed clean of sins.'[3]

Third, submersion is a fuller ritual enactment of baptism's meanings than any other mode.[4]
Prior to the post-Reformation period, aspersion (sprinkling) was not used except for clinical baptism. The experience of being sprinkled with a few drops of water does not communicate any of the layers of baptism's meanings—not cleansing, not birth, certainly not death and burial. Is God's grace so minimal that Christians can be satisfied with sprinkling?

Nearly the same is true of affusion (pouring). What is its sign value? It cannot express birth or death, and it is impossible even to bathe with only three handsful (or shellsful) of water.

Immersion, whether by pouring water over the head of someone who is standing or kneeling in water, or by partially lowering an infant into the water, suggests baptism's meaning as bathing. However, immersion is not able to communicate either the birth or paschal meanings of water.

---

[1] *Worship in the New Testament*, Part ii (Grove Liturgical Study 12-13, Grove Books, Bramcote, Notts., 1978), p.52.

[2] *Baptism in the New Testament* (SCM Press, London, 1960), Westminster Press edition, p.22.

[3] *The Babylonian Captivity of the Church*, in Abdel Ross Wentz, (ed.), *Luther's Works*, Volume 36 (Fortress Press, Philadelphia, 1959), p.68.

[4] See chapter 1 regarding the various modes of baptism, and especially the difference between immersion and submersion.

Only submersion—in which the entire body is completely under the water—has the sign value of drowning, of death, of burial and resurrection with Christ. The point is not how much water is necessary for baptism to be efficacious, but rather how much water it takes for both neophytes and congregations to realize the radical nature of baptism. Certainly the omnipotent God can effect salvation when only a few drops of water are used. However, if the Church is to recover the full and profound significance of baptism, then baptism must be done in a way that is consistent with its meaning: submersion in abundant water. In his *Large Catechism*, Luther wrote that baptism

'consists of being dipped into the water, which covers us completely, and being drawn out again. These two parts, being dipped under the water and emerging from it, indicate the power and effect of baptism, which is simply the slaying of the Old Adam and the resurrection of the new man.'[1]

Perhaps a congregation can only comprehend baptism as death and resurrection if the font holds enough water that an adult *could* drown. Does not the meaning of baptism deserve and indeed demand that kind of architectural and ritual radicality?

The preference for submersion is not novel for Anglicans:

'The first method of baptizing which the Church of England acknowledges (and this has always been the case) is submersion. It stands there in the rubric [in the *Alternative Service Book*], and has been a continuous witness from the days of Anglo-Saxon baptisms in rivers to Norman fonts which can still be seen today and are large enough to dip a baby, and from the days of Cranmer's Prayer Books which explicitly required submersion . . . right through to *ASB 1980* which makes it the first choice still.'[2]

In the current Roman Catholic adult baptismal rite, the rubrics prefer 'immersion,' which is defined as being 'of the whole body or of the head only'.[3] Thus the acts of submersion and immersion are combined in the term *immersion*. The same mode is specified for children of catechetical age.

Fourth, fonts are for the baptism of adults as well as infants.
While, without a doubt, the majority of baptisms in liturgical churches are of infants, adult baptisms are occurring in growing numbers. But will adult baptism ever be taken seriously by the Church, or by the adult candidates, until once again fonts are provided which enable adult submersion? It is a ritual and symbolic contradiction of the meaning of baptism to require an adult to bend over a font which looks like a birdbath.

---

[1] Section 4; in Theodore G. Tappert (trans. and ed.), *The Book of Concord: The Confessions of the Evangelical Lutheran Church* (Fortress Press, Philadelphia, 1959), pp.444-445.

[2] Colin Buchanan, in Buchanan, Trevor Lloyd, and Harold Miller (eds.), *Anglican Worship Today* (Collins, London, 1980), pp.169-170. Regarding Anglican fonts (in England and Wales) designed for adult immersion and submersion, see Brandwood.

[3] International Commission on English in the Liturgy, and U.S. Bishops' Committee on the Liturgy, *Rite of Christian Initiation of Adults*, p.142.

Certainly infant baptisms will continue, but that should not control people's understanding of the meaning of the sacrament. If the baptismal paradigm shifts from its birth orientation to the paschal, baptism can be liberated from its bondage to the trivial and minimal. With fonts large enough and deep enough for adult submersion, the Church can be freed from symbolic and ritual bankruptcy. Even if a given parish does not currently practise submersion of adults, an ample font would make it possible in the future.

THE DESIGN OF FONTS
Size
The pre-eminent symbol of baptism is living water, for which the font functions as container. The most important quality of the font is, therefore, the amount of water it holds. At the most minimal, a font should hold enough water for the immersion of infants; as a rule of thumb, that means a font 1 metre across, with water at least .50 metres deep. Ideally, however, a font should be large enough to accommodate the submersion of adults as well as infants. Thus, a general guideline is 2.50 metres across, with water about 1 metre deep.

The font at the new St. Benedict Church[1] (*Illustration 1*) in Chicago is 7.30 metres in diameter; at its deepest, the water is about 1 metre deep. It holds nearly

Illustration 1 — St. Benedict the African, Chicago.

[1] James J. Belli, architect; Regina Kuehn, liturgical design consultant.

38,000 litres of water, and has seven broad steps. Located in an African-American parish, the font was designed to reflect the traditional African respect for the earth, and thus is round, to resemble a natural pool of water.[1]

A large font/pool makes a visual statement about the meaning and importance of baptism. Large submersion pools communicate symbolic intensity; in holding enough water to drown or bathe in, they help people enlarge and deepen their understanding of baptism as burial with Christ and as salvific washing in the Triune Name.

Adults and Infants

It is a challenge to design fonts which enable both adult and infant baptism by immersion or submersion. Some modern fonts have two or more levels of water, usually a raised area for infants and a separate lower pool for adults. But these multi-level pools may tend to suggest that infant baptism is fundamentally different from adult baptism. That, in turn, may be an inadvertent contradiction of the fact that 'there is one Lord, one faith, one Baptism' (Ephesians 4.5).

The cruciform font at St. Charles Borromeo Church[2] (*Illustration 2*) in London suggests a way to provide a pool which can serve for both infant and adult baptism. Built in the 1982 renovation of an old inner-city church, the sunken pool is

Illustration 2 — St. Charles Borromeo, London.

---

[1] For more on this font, see Baldwin; and Kuehn, pp.45-50. Also see below, under 'Location.'

[2] Michael Anderson, architect. This font is modelled after one in Madrid, designed by Kiko Arguello.

cruciform, 3.65 metres across, set within an octagonal rim. The adult candidate descends into the waters of death with Christ and then rises into new life. (*Illustration 3*) By going down the steps on one side and coming up on the opposite side, there is the experience of baptism as a passage from one life into another, similar to the Israelites' passage through the Red Sea from slavery into freedom. This font enables linear as well as vertical movement: descent, submersion, passage, and ascent. The square crossing area at its centre can be isolated by plate glass panels, so that only the centre needs to be filled with water for infant baptism, thus precluding the necessity of the priest also being in the water.[1]

Illustration 3 — St. Charles Borromeo, London.

Shape

The shape of a font is important symbolically and pedagogically. Many fonts which are of non-symbolic shapes look more like they belong in shopping malls or spas or gardens, than in churches; they are incapable of evoking baptismal

[1] For more on this font, see Nugent. Also, see below, under 'Covers.'

imagery. Indeed, they are more likely to evoke thoughts of luxury and consumerism, thus contradicting the counter-cultural nature of Christianity ('Do not be conformed to this world . . .' Romans 12.2).

Based on the paschal paradigm for baptism, cruciform fonts most immediately 'speak' the meaning of this sacrament. This seems particularly important in modern Western culture where the denial of death is pervasive, and in an age when the scandal of the cross is less appealing to many people than cheap grace.

In recent research on Anglican worship in inner-city England, it was found that 'some in the inner city felt that the *Alternative Service Book* was too triumphalistic, with too much use of resurrection imagery. What they wanted . . . was something that reflected a little more realistically the pain of the cross.'[1] Cruciform fonts can speak clearly that baptism is the sacrament of the cross.

Outstanding cruciform fonts, both built in the ground and set within octagonal rims, were built in renovations of two inner-city churches in London: St. Charles Borromeo (in 1982; see above), and Guardian Angel Church[2] (in 1988). (*Colour plate 3*)

Another in-ground cruciform font was built in 1986 in St. Francis of Assisi Church, Concord, California.[3] (*Illustration 4*) This pool is approximately 2

Illustration 4 — St. Francis of Assisi, Concord, CA.

---

[1] Trevor Lloyd, 'Inner City England,' in David R. Holeton, ed., *Liturgical Inculturation in the Anglican Communion* (Alcuin/GROW Joint Liturgical Study no. 15, Grove Books, Bramcote, Notts., 1990), p.43.
[2] Mottio Del Prete, architect.
[3] Frank Mighetto, architect.

metres across, with water about .75 metres deep. On opposite sides of the cross, there are three steps into and out of the water. The pool is faced with blue ceramic tile.[1]

In 1993 a large above-ground cruciform font was constructed at the new Lutheran Church of the Redeemer, Chimacum, Washington.[2] ((*Colour plate 4*) Holding approximately 500 gallons of water, it is about 2 metres across and 1 metre deep, and has two steps on each of two opposite interior sides. Two sets of oak steps are placed on the exterior of the font when there are baptisms, one set for entrance into the pool, and the other on the opposite side for exit. The water is heated and re-circulated. The font is constructed of poured concrete and faced with native stone on the exterior and waterproof plaster on the interior.

Illustration 5 — Anglican Cathedral, Portsmouth.

A different type of cruciform font has been constructed in the reordering of the Anglican Cathedral in Portsmouth, England.[3] (*Illustration 5*) It is above-ground, with one interior step on each side, and an interior depth of .56 metres. The exterior of the font is nearly 1.70 metres long and 1.15 metres wide. It enables both infant and adult immersion without the presider being in the water. A valve in the drain (at the bottom centre) permits both filling and draining.

Octagonal fonts also symbolize the paschal (death and resurrection) meaning of baptism, although they take far more catechesis than the cross-

---

[1] For more on this font, see Stauffer (1988), pp.24-27.
[2] Designed by Lou Hefner of the parish.
[3] Michael Drury, architect; David Stancliffe, liturgical consultant.

shape itself. It is ideal if octagonal fonts have steps on opposite sides, enabling the sense of passage through the waters, as well as descent and ascent.

An above-ground octagonal pool was constructed in the 1986 renovation[1] of Saints Peter and Paul Cathedral in Indianapolis, Indiana. This font is about 1.70 metres across, with water approximately .50 metres deep. It must be entered via a portable stile (set of steps).[2]

The octagonal font at St. Monica Church[3] in Chicago is 2.40 metres across. It has interior steps on only one side (see pages 54-55 below).

Covers

The cruciform font at St. Charles Borromeo Church (see above) can be covered with sections of brass-faced timber, so that a coffin can be set on it for a funeral. (*Illustration 6*) Again, the paschal meaning of baptism is made clear, and a visual connection is immediately made between baptismal death and earthly death. The sections of the cover serve as an altar frontal at all times except when there is a funeral in the church. Thus, a visual connection is also made between baptism and eucharist. (Whether this practice works well, however, depends on the location of the font.)

Illustration 6 — St. Charles Borromeo, London.

---

[1] Edward A. Sövik, architect. See also below, under 'Covers'.
[2] For more on this font, see Stauffer (1988), pp.23-24.
[3] John C. Voosen, architect; Regina Kuehn, liturgical design consultant. See also below, under 'Location.'

Fonts do not otherwise need covers and, in fact, should not be covered. When people come into the church, they should be able both to see and to touch the water.

In some places, however, insurance regulations or municipal laws may make it necessary to prevent accidental drowning of children. In those situations it is necessary to design safeguarding devices which neither detract from the symbolism of the font nor make the water inaccessible. The octagonal font at the Cathedral of Saints Peter and Paul in Indianapolis (see above) can be safeguarded with a brass wire 'fishnet', hooked into the interior of the pool about 2 centimetres below the surface of the water. It is easily removed when baptism is celebrated.

Another approach to prevention of drowning was taken at Redeemer, Chimacum, Washington (see above): short table-like clear plexiglass inserts are placed below the water surface when there are no baptisms. They are virtually invisible and easily removable. Bubbles are prevented by the use of a de-bubbling solution made for hot tubs.

LOCATION

The font is a part of the worship space, not a furnishing set in it. It is best to think of the font in architectonic terms, not as a piece of furniture. Likewise, the font should be located in its own defined space, just as the altar has its own defined space. It should be visible and accessible to the worshipping assembly. Finally, it is important that the space around the font be adequate both for people to gather around it for the sacramental celebration, as well as for other liturgical purposes. In addition, provision should be made near the font for placement of the oil (chrism) and the paschal candle.

The location of the font makes a theological statement—preferably a statement of baptism as entrance into the community of believers. The most meaningful (and a very practical) location is just inside the main entrance to the nave.

The baptistery at St. Monica Church (see above) in Chicago is located perfectly. (*Illustration 7*) The people enter the building into a spacious narthex or gathering area. The baptistery is between the narthex and the nave, with no barriers between these three spaces. Baptism is symbolized not only as entrance, but also as liminality, as threshold. The baptistery itself is octagonal, evocative of early Christian baptisteries such as that in Milan. Clerestory windows make it a light space in the daytime, and the stained glass wall splashes colour across the entire baptistery, including the water. The font must be passed in order to enter the nave, and the font is on axis with the altar, thus making a good visual and theological connection between baptism and eucharist. The baptistery is a well-defined space, yet it is functionally a part of the worship space.

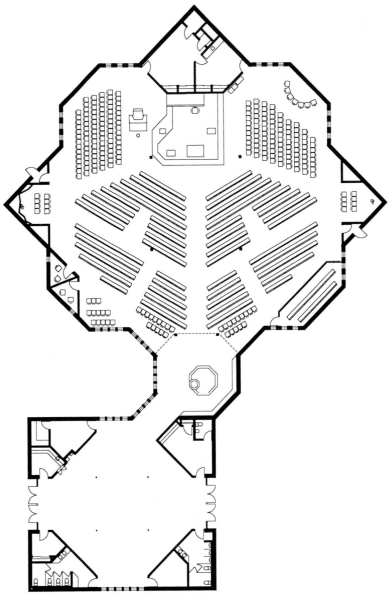

Illustration 7 — St. Monica, Chicago.

Another excellent entrance location (*Illustration 8*) is at St. Benedict the African in Chicago (see above). After entering the church building, the people walk up a curving and sloping hallway, and then around the large baptismal pool, before going into the worship space. The baptistery, the pool, and the worship space are all round, and the pool is on axis with the altar. When there is a baptism, the congregation literally surrounds the font, providing a 'communal embrace' of the neophyte.

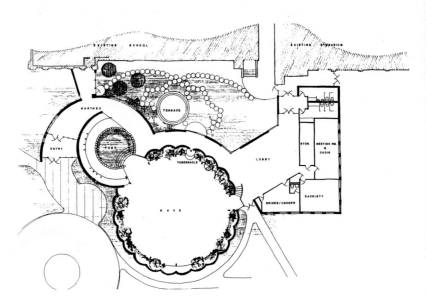

Illustration 8 — St. Benedict the African, Chicago.

ICONOGRAPHY
Iconography is one means of calling attention to the font, as well as of visually proclaiming the meanings of baptism. The corners of the fonts at St. Charles Borromeo Church and Guardian Angel Church, both in London, contain symbols of the four evangelists in mosaic. The stained glass baptistery wall at St. Monica Church[1], Chicago, depicts water and aquatic life, and the glass is low enough that children can look directly at the water and fish imagery as they walk through the baptistery. Images of biblical 'water' narratives might also be put on a canopy over the font, as was done at St. Hugo of the Hills Church in Bloomfield Hills, Michigan.[2]

---

[1] Robert Harmon, stained-glass artist.
[2] Robert E. Rambusch, designer.

It is better if decoration of fonts is limited to images, because they are multivalent and have evocative power. The use of words is discouraged because they are more cerebral than evocative.

TEMPORARY FONTS FOR THE EASTER VIGIL

In parishes where it is impossible to install a significant font which will accommodate adult submersion, temporary fonts can be constructed easily and inexpensively for use annually at the Easter Vigil. Another use of such temporary fonts is in parishes considering renovation or new construction, in which a font for immersion or submersion is proposed.

It is important to determine in advance that the floor where the temporary font is to be located is solid enough to bear the water's weight.

Perhaps the easiest way to provide a temporary font is to borrow an oblong watering tank for farm animals, although this requires thoughtful covering and decoration.

It is relatively simple to construct a rectangular font of wood or concrete blocks which has the appearance of a coffin. Waterproofing can be provided by several swimming-pool liners.

However, the paschal meaning of Baptism is clearer to neophytes and congregation alike if a cruciform font is built out of concrete blocks, and waterproofed with pool liners.[1]

With any of these, consideration should be given to making the bottom of the pool slip-proof. In addition, the appearance deserves careful thought, so that it does not distract from the sacramental purpose. Temporary fonts can be filled with warm water using simple garden hoses, and can be drained by a siphon or with a small pump. It is important to be sure the sides and ends of the font are sturdy enough to withstand the heavy weight and pressure of the water. It is wise to wrap the sides of concrete-block or wooden fonts with two steel bands.

PRACTICALITIES

Steps

Steps within fonts are both utilitarian and symbolic. They enable entrance into and exit from the water, in a way which allows the candidate to descend into death and burial with Christ, and then ascend into new life in him. Often the number of steps has been interpreted with additional symbolism, but perhaps it is better simply to let them provide the experience of going down and coming up.

Two sets of steps should be provided within opposite sides of fonts, thus enabling the neophyte actually to pass through the baptismal waters. (See *Illustration 3*)

---

[1] For a description and photos of one such temporary cruciform font, see Marchal and Conrad.

If the font is above-ground, two portable sets of steps are placed at opposite exterior sides of the font on days when there are baptisms. (*Illustration 9*)

Illustration 9 — Redeemer, Chimacum, WA.

For safety, non-slip surfaces should be used for steps. However, it is best, for symbolic and aesthetic reasons, to avoid handrails. If assistance is needed, let it be provided by a minister, sponsor, or another member of the congregation, as an enactment of human support within the body of Christ.

Floor
The floor surrounding the font must be impervious to water; therefore, wood and/or carpet surfaces are not advised.

In addition, the surface should not be slippery. Water splashed on a polished marble or terrazzo floor, for example, renders it extremely hazardous for walking. Surfaces with some texture are better than highly polished floors.

Changing Rooms
When adult immersion and/or submersion is practised, nearby changing rooms are needed, perhaps for the presider as well as the neophytes. The entire floor between the font and the changing rooms, as well as within the changing rooms themselves, should be water-resistant and non-slippery. It is helpful to provide towels, mirrors, combs, and perhaps hairdryers. If properly located, restrooms can serve as changing rooms.

Plumbing

Fonts large enough for adult submersion require several types of plumbing equipment. First, a pumping system is needed to fill and drain the font. Both for good maintenance access, and for noise prevention, it is best if the pump and its controls are a distance from the font itself.

Second, a decision must be made whether or not the font will have re-circulating water. Some congregations and architects prefer to avoid the symbolism of re-circulating the water in which God's grace is bestowed. In other situations, water conservation is more important. Third, it is desirable for the water actually to move within the font (whether or not it is re-cycled). This can be accomplished by various means of aeration or by a small pump.

Fourth is the need for heating the water to a comfortable level prior to the celebration of a baptism. Fifth, it is necessary to determine whether the water needs to be filtered, whether it needs to be purified, and how to keep the font clean from algae and other impurities. Depending on the water source, a wide variety of methods is possible.

RITUAL MATTERS

Mode

Chapter 1 describes various modes of baptism in history, and the difference between submersion and immersion.

Illustration 10 — St. Charles Borromeo, London.

Both submersion and immersion require a sense of grace and deliberateness on the part of the presiding minister. It is not inappropriate to suggest pastors and priests should practise these acts well in advance, until the mechanics of the movements are mastered, so that the movements can be graceful and unhurried when done within the actual sacramental setting. Perhaps this is particularly true for clergy inexperienced in handling infants.

Submersion of adults can be done several ways, depending on the depth of the water in the font. If the font is deep enough, the presider may stand slightly to the rear of the candidate, place his/her arm across the candidate's upper back, and lower the candidate backwards completely under the water. (*Illustration 10*) If it is easier, the candidate may be lowered frontwards, completely under the water.

If the water is not deep enough for the candidate to stand, he or she may kneel, and be lowered forward by the presider, until the candidate's head is completely under the water.

Immersion of adults can also be done in a variety of ways, with the candidate either standing or kneeling in the water. The presider may pour a generous amount of water over the head (perhaps using a large ewer or pitcher), or the presider may push the candidate's head forwards, partially into the water.

In the West, infants are submersed horizontally; in the East, infant submersion is done vertically. In either case, the infant is lowered completely under the water.

Some parents will be more comfortable with immersion of infants, rather than submersion. The presider may hold the infant, lowering both body and head partially into the water as the formula is spoken. Or, a parent or sponsor may hold the infant partially in the water, as the presider scoops water over the head while speaking the formula.

Whether submersion or immersion, with adults or infants, the action normally is repeated three times (once at the naming of each person of the Trinity in the baptismal formula), although this depends on the rite in use.

Clothing for Candidates and Presiders

For either submersion or immersion, infants are baptized naked (although it might prove wise to use a lightweight cloth diaper or a rubber pant with a male infant).

Adult candidates are modestly and practically clothed. Skirts should be avoided. Both men and women may wear washable slacks and simple short-sleeved shirts, preferably in dark colours (thus providing a contrast with the white post-baptismal garment). Obviously, candidates are to be barefoot.

As the neophytes leave the water, they may be dried with large, thick white towels, and then enrobed in white garments (preferably made of relatively heavy fabric). In some churches, the presentation of the baptismal garment is accompanied by a text about its meaning.[1] Thus, the white garment has both practical and symbolic functions; its use can be traced to the early Church, and it has reference to Galatians 3.27 and Revelation 7.9.

If the design of the font is such that the presiding minister also enters the water, his or her alb should be of heavy washable fabric and should have weights sewn into the hem.

---

[1] The American *Lutheran Book of Worship* (1978) rubrics call for a representative of the congregation to say 'Put on this robe, for in Baptism you have been clothed in the righteousness of Christ, who calls you to his great feast.' (However, the presentation of the garment is too late in the rite to be practical if submersion or immersion has been used.) The Roman Catholic Rite of Christian Initiation of Adults (1988) specifies that while the godparents place the garment on the newly baptized, the presider says 'You have become a new creation and have clothed yourselves in Christ. Receive this baptismal garment and bring it unstained to the judgment seat of our Lord Jesus Christ, so that you may have everlasting life.'

A time needs to be provided after the baptisms for neophytes (and the pre-sider, if he/she has entered the water) to change into dry clothing. (See section on changing rooms, above.) During this time, the congregation may sing hymns. After changing, neophytes remain clothed in the white baptismal garments through the conclusion of the liturgy.

CONCLUSION

The sacrament of holy baptism is a profound and radical act—profound because it draws us deeply into Christ and the paschal mystery, and radical because it grafts us onto the very roots of the Christian faith and into the body of Christ.

Baptism is simultaneously a cosmic and an individual act—because it makes each of us a part of salvation history. It is a profoundly personal act with radical corporate consequences—because it makes each of us a child of God, while at the same time incorporating us into the whole communion of saints of every time and every place.

Baptism is a termination and a new beginning—because it is the death of our old selves, and the beginning of life in Christ and his Church. The waters which drown us are also the waters which give us new life. In passing through the waters of the font, we take up the cross of Christ; but at the same time, Christ gives us proleptic entrance into Paradise.

Font designs based on such theology can result in fonts which are worthy of their holy purpose, and which will in themselves be instrumental in ongoing spiritual formation.

Bibliography

Alexander, Margaret, 'Design and Meaning in the Early Christian Mosaics of Tunisia' in *Apollo* (1983), pp.8-13.

_____, 'The Symbolism of Christianity' in *Archaeology* (Winter·1950), pp.242-247.

Ariarajah, Wesley, 'The Water of Life' in *Ecumenical Review*, 34:3 (July 1982), pp.271-279.

Babelon, E., *et al.*, *Atlas archéologique de la Tunisie* (Second edition, Paris, 1920).

Baldwin, David, 'There Is a Sweet, Sweet Spirit in This Place' in *Faith and Form*, XXV (Fall 1991), pp.24-26.

Baucheron, Fr. et R. Colardelle, 'Le baptistère et la topographie de Grenoble aux premiers temps chrétiens' in *Bulletin* (L'Association pour l'Antiquité tardive), 2 (Annuaire 1992), pp.32-36.

Beasley-Murray, G. R., *Baptism in the New Testament*, (William B. Eerdmans Publishing Co., Grand Rapids, Michigan, 1962).

Bedard, Walter M. *The Symbolism of the Baptismal Font in Early Christian Thought* (The Catholic University of America Press, Washington, D. C., 1951).

Bejaoui, Fathi, 'Découvertes d'archéologie chrétienne en Tunisie' in *Actes du XIe congrès international d'archéologie chrétienne*, Vol. II (Lyon, Vienne, Grenoble, Genève et Aoste, 1986) (Pontificio Istituto di Archeologia Cristiana, Roma, 1989), pp.1927-1959.

_____, 'Documents d'archéologie et d'épigraphie paléochrétiennes récemment découverts en Tunisie, dans la région de Jilma' in *Comptes rendus des séances de l'Académie des Inscriptions et Belles-Lettres* (1990), pp.256-277.

_____, 'Nouvelles découvertes chrétiennes dans les régions de Thelepte et de Jilma et à propos d'une coupe en bronze a décor biblique' in *Bulletin de Travaux de l'Institut d'Archéologie et d'Art, Comptes Rendus* (Avril-Juin 1988), pp.17-34.

Benoît, Fernand, *Cimiez: La ville antique* (Ed. E. de Boccard, Paris, 1977).

Bertelli, Carlo, *et al.*, *Milano, una capitale da Ambrogio ai Carolingi* (Edizioni Electa, Milano, 1987).

Beschaouch, Azedine, *et al.*, *Les ruines de Bulla Regia* (École Française, Rome, 1977).

Bethune, Ade, 'The Primacy of the Font' in *Sacred Signs*, 4:1 (Michaelmas 1980), pp.2-9.

Bognetti, Gian Piero, *Castelseprio, Artistic and Historical Guide* (2nd. ed. Neri Pozza Editore, Vicenza, 1968).

Bond, Francis, *Fonts and Font Covers* (Oxford University Press, London, 1908. Reprinted 1985, with new topographical index, by Waterstone & Co., London).

Bonnet, Charles, 'Baptistères et groupes épiscopaux d'Aoste et de Genève, évolution architecturale et aménagements liturgiques' in *Actes du XIe congrès international d'archéologie chrétienne*, Vol. II (Lyon, Vienne, Grenoble, Genève et Aoste, 1986) (Pontificio Istituto di Archeologie Cristiana, Roma, 1989), pp.1407-1426.

———, *Geneva in Early Christian Times* (Geneva, 1986).

———, 'Saint-Pierre de Genève, recentes découvertes archéologiques' in *Archéologie suisse*, Vol. 3, No. 4 (1980), pp.174-191.

———, and Renato Perinetti, *Aoste: aux premiers temps chrétiens* (Musumeci Editeur, Aoste, Italy, 1986).

Bovini, Giuseppi, *Ravenna: Its Mosaics and Monuments* (A. Longo Editore, Ravenna, 1980).

Bradshaw, Paul, *The Search for the Origins of Christian Worship* (SPCK, London, 1992). Chapter 7: 'Christian Initiation, A Study in Diversity'.

Brandwood, G. K., 'Immersion Baptistries in Anglican Churches' in *Archaeological Journal*, 147 (1990), pp.420-436.

Brivio, Ernesto, *Guide of the Duomo of Milan* (Veneranda Fabbrica of the Duomo, Milano, 1978).

Brown, Henry F., *Baptism through the Centuries* (Pacific Press, Mountain View, California, 1965).

Brusin, Giovanni, *Aquileia e Grado* (Edizione secunda, Tip. Antoniana, Padua, Italy, 1952).

Buhler, F. M. *Archéologie et bapteme, évolution du baptême et des installations baptismales* (Centre de Culture Chrétienne, Mulhouse, 1986).

———, 'Occupation romaine des régions rhénanes et questions posées par les installations baptismales des ouvrages militaires' in *Bulletin du Musée historique et des sciences humaines de Mulhouse*, Tome XCI (1984).

Burnish, Raymond, *The Meaning of Baptism: A Comparison of the Teaching and Practice of the Fourth Century with the Present Day* (Alcuin Club Collection No. 67. Alcuin Club/SPCK, London, 1985).

Cabrol, F., H. LeClerc, and H. Marrou, *Dictionnaire d'archéologie chrétienne et de la liturgie* (Librairie Letouzey et Ané, Paris, 1924-1953). (See articles on individual sites.)

Cameron, Averil, 'Byzantine Africa, The Literary Evidence' in *Excavations at Carthage 1978 Conducted by the University of Michigan*. Vol. VII. Edited by J. H. Humphrey (Kelsey Museum, University of Michigan, Ann Arbor, Michigan, 1982).

Canby, Courtlandt, *A Guide to the Archaeological Sites of Israel, Egypt and North Africa* (Facts on File, New York, 1990).

Chapman, Michael Andrew, 'The Liturgical Directions of Saint Charles Borromeo, The Baptistery' in *Liturgical Arts*, 24:1 (November 1955), 13-15.

Cintas, J., and N. Duval, 'L'église du prêtre Felix (région de Kélibia)' in *Karthago*, IX (1958), pp.155-265.

Clover, Frank, 'Carthage and the Vandals' in *Excavations at Carthage 1978 Conducted by the University of Michigan*. Vol. VII. Edited by J. H. Humphrey (Kelsey Museum, University of Michigan, Ann Arbor, Michigan, 1982).

Colombo, Silvano, and Gianfranco Garancini, *Il Battistero: Note storiche ed artistiche per la conoscenza dei monumenti varesini* (Edizioni Lativa, Varese, 1981).

Corbett, G. U. S, 'A Note on the Arrangement of the Early Christian Buildings at Aquileia' in *Rivista di archeologia cristiana*, 32 (1956), pp.99-106.

Cote, Wolfred Nelson, *The Archaeology of Baptism* (Yates and Alexander, London, 1876).

Courtois, Christian, 'Sur un baptistère découvert dans la région de Kélibia' in *Karthago*, VI (1955), pp.97-127.

Cramer, Peter, *Baptism and Change in the Early Middle Ages, c. 200-c. 1150* (Cambridge University Press, Cambridge, 1993).

Cuscito, Giuseppe, *Die Basilika von Aquileia* (La Fotocromo Emiliana, Bologna, 1978).

_____, *Die Früchristlichen Basiliken von Grado* (Specimen Grafica Editoriale, Bologna, 1979).

Danielou, Jean, *Primitive Christian Symbols*. Translated by Donald Atwater. (Helicon Press, Baltimore, 1964).

_____, and Marrou, Henri, *The Christian Centuries, The First Six Hundred Years* (Darton, Longman and Todd, London, 1979).

David-Roy, Marguerite, 'Les baptistères de la Gaule' in *Archéologie*, No. 135 (10/1979), pp.51-59.

Davies, J. G., *The Architectural Setting of Baptism* (Barrie and Rockliff, London, 1962).

_____, *The Origin and Development of Early Christian Church Architecture* (SCM Press Ltd., London, 1952).

De Bruyne, L, 'La décoration des baptistères paléo-chrétiens' in *Miscellanea Liturgica in honorem L. C. Mohlberg* (Roma, 1948), pp.189ff.

Deichmann, F. W., 'Baptisterium' in (T. Klauser ed.), *Reallexikon für Antike und Christentum* (Hiersemann, Stuttgart, 1950). Vol. I, cols. 1157-1167.

Dölger, F. J., 'Zur Symbolik des altchristlichen Taufhauses' in *Antike und Christentum*, IV (1934), pp.153-187.

D'Ossat, G. de Angelis, 'L'architettura ambrosiana ed il Battistero di Fréjus' in *VIII Corso di Cultura sull'Arte Ravennate e Bizantina* (Ravenna, 1961).

Drewer, Lois, 'Fisherman and Fish Pond, From the Sea of Sin to the Living Waters' in *The Art Bulletin*, LXIII:4 (December 1981), pp.533-547.

Duval, Noel, *Basiliques chrétiennes d'Afrique du Nord*. I, *Inventaire de l'Algérie*. Tome 1, Texte; Tome 2, Illustrations (Institut d'Études Augustiniennes, Paris, 1992).

_____, 'Église et temple en Afrique du Nord' in *Bulletin archéologique du Comité des travaux historiques et scientifiques*, nouvelle série, 7, année 1971 (Paris, 1973), pp.265-296.

_____, 'Études d'archéologie chrétienne nord-africaine, XVII—Une nouvelle cuve baptismale dans le centre de Carthage' in *Revue des études Augustiniennes*, 34 (1988), pp.86-92.

_____, 'Études d'architecture chrétienne nord-africaine' in *Mélanges de d'école française de Rome; Antiquite*, Tome 84:2 (1972), pp.1071-1097.

_____, 'Les baptistères d'Acholla (Tunisie) et l'origine des baptistères polylobes en Afrique du Nord' in *Antiquites africaines*, 15 (1980), pp.329-343.

_____, *Les églises africaines à deux absides*. Tome I, *Les basiliques de Sbeitla*. Tome II, *Inventaire des monuments—interpretation* (Editions E. de Boccard, Paris, 1971 (Tome I) and 1973 (Tome II)).

_____, 'L'évêque et la cathédrale en Afrique du Nord' in *Actes du XIe congrés international d'archéologie chrétienne* (Lyon, Vienne, Grenoble, Genève et Aoste, 1986) (Pontificio Istituto di Archeologie Cristiana, Roma, 1989), pp.345-399.

_____, and François Baratte, *Les ruines de Sufetula: Sbeitla* (Societé Tunisienne de Diffusion, Tunis, 1973).

_____, and Jean Guyon, 'Le baptistère en Occident' in *La Maison-Dieu*, No. 193 (1993), pp.53-70.

_____, and Alexandre Lézine, 'Nécropole chrétienne et baptistère souterrain a Carthage' in *Cahiers archéologiques*, X (1959), pp.71-147.

Emminghaus, Johannes H, 'Semiotik altchristlicher Taufhaeuser' in *Zeitschrift für Katholische Theologie*, 107:1-2 (1985), pp.39-51.

Ennabli, Liliane, 'La Basilique de Carthagenna' in *Pour Sauver Carthage*. Dir. by Abdelmajid Ennabli (UNESCO et L'Institut National d'Archéologie et d'Art, Tunis, 1992).

Eyice, Semavi, 'Un baptistère byzantin a side en Pamphylie' in *Actes du Ve congrès international d'archéologie chrétienne* (Aix-en-Provence, 1954) (Pontificio Istituto di Archeologia Cristiana, Roma, 1957).

Fausone, Alfonso M. *Die Taufe in der Frühchristlichen Sepulkralkunst* (Pontificio Istituto di Archeologia Cristiana, Roma, 1982).

Fendri, Mohamed, *Basiliques chrétiennes de la Skhira* (Presses Universitaires de France, Paris, 1961).

Fête, Joseph N, 'The Cultural Background of the Roman Ritual of Baptism' (Unpublished S.T.M. thesis, Yale University Divinity School, 1981).

Février, Paul-Albert, 'L'abeille et la seiche, à propos du décor du baptistère de Kélibia' in *Rivista di archeologia christiana*, LX:3-4 (1984), pp.277-292.

_____, *Le groupe épiscopal de Fréjus* (Editions de la Caisse Nationale des Monuments Historiques et des Sites, Paris, 1981).

_____, 'Les quatre fleuves du Paradis' in *Rivista di archeologia cristiana*, 32 (1956), pp.179-199.

_____, 'Les baptistères de Provence pendant le moyen age' in *Actes du Ve congrès international d'archéologie chrétienne* (Aix-en-Provence, 1954) (Pontificio Istituto di Archeologie Cristiana, Roma, 1957), pp.423-432.

Février, P.-A., and C. Poinssot, 'Les cierges et l'abeille, Note sur l'iconographie du baptistère découvert dans la région de Kélibia (Tunisie)' in *Cahiers archéologiques*, X (1959), pp.149-156.

Finn, Thomas M, *Early Christian Baptism and the Catechumenate: Italy, North Africa, and Egypt* (Liturgical Press, Collegeville, Minnesota, 1992).

Fisher, J. D. C., *Christian Initiation: Baptism in the Medieval West: A Study in the Disintegration of the Primitive Rite of Initiation* (Alcuin Club Collections No. XLVII. SPCK, London, 1965).

Frend, W. H. C., 'The Early Christian Church in Carthage' in *Excavations at Carthage 1976 Conducted by the University of Michigan* (University of Michigan, Ann Arbor, Michigan, 1977).

———, *The Rise of Christianity* (Fortress Press, Philadelphia, 1984).

Gauckler, Paul, *Basiliques chrétiennes de Tunisie* (Paris, 1913).

Gigli, Laura, *San Marcello al Corso* (Istituto di Studi Romani, Roma, 1977).

Giovenale, Giovanni, *Il Battistero Lateranense*. Studia di Antichita Cristiana, Vol. I. (Pontificio Istituto di Archeologia Cristiana, Roma, 1929).

Goettelmann, Paul A., *The Baptistery of Fréjus* (The Catholic University of America Press, Washington, D.C., 1933).

Grabar, André, *Christian Iconography, A Study of Its Origins* (Princeton University Press, Princeton, New Jersey, 1968).

———, 'Le baptistère paléochrétien, les problems que pose l'étude des baptistères paléochrétiennes' in *Actes du Ve congrès international d'archeologie chrétienne* (Aix-en-Provence, 1954) (Pontificio Istituto di Archéologie Cristiana, Roma, 1957).

Green, E. Tyrell, *Baptismal Fonts* (SPCK, London, 1928).

Grün, Anselm, *Taufstätten* (Echter, Wurzburg, 1988).

Guyon, Jean, 'Baptistères et groupes épiscopaux de Provence' in *Actes du XIe congrès international d'archéologie chrétienne*, Vol. II (Lyon, Vienne, Grenoble, Genève et Aoste, 1986) (Pontificio Istituto di Archeologie Cristiana, Roma, 1989), pp.1427-1449.

———, 'Le baptême et ses monuments' in *Naissance des arts chrétiens* (Atlas des Monuments Palochrétiens de la France. Ministere de la Culture et de la Communication, Paris, 1991).

Humphrey, John H, 'Pied du versant est de Byrsa, l'évolution d'un quartier' in *Pour Sauver Carthage*. Dir. by Abdelmajid Ennabli (UNESCO et L'Institut National d'Archologie et d'Art, Tunis, 1992).

International Commission on English in the Liturgy, and U.S. Bishops' Committee on the Liturgy, *Rite of Christian Initiation of Adults* (Liturgy Training Publications, Chicago, 1988).

Jannet-Vallat, Monique, Roger Lauxerois, and Jean-Francois Reynaud, *Vienne aux premiers temps chrétiens* (Patrimoine Rhonalpin, Lyon, 1986).

Kavanagh, Aidan, 'Symbolic Implications of Christian Initiation in Roman Catholicism since the Second Vatican Council' in *I Simboli dell'iniziazione Christiana* (Benedictina-Edizioni Abbazia S. Paolo, Roma, 1983).

———, *The Shape of Baptism, The Rite of Christian Initiation* (Pueblo Publishing Company, New York, 1978).

Khatchatrian, A., *Les baptistères paléochrétiens*. (Paris, 1962).

———, *Origine et typologie des baptistères paléochrétiens* (Centre de Culture Chrétienne, Mulhouse, France, 1982).

Kostof, Spiro, *The Orthodox Baptistery of Ravenna* (Yale University Press, New Haven, Connecticut, 1965).

Kraeling, Carl H, 'The Christian Building' in *The Excavations at Dura-Europos: Final Report VIII, Part II.* Edited by C. Bradford Welles (Dura-Europos Publications, New Haven, Connecticut, 1967).

Krautheimer, Richard, *Early Christian and Byzantine Architecture* (Fourth edition, Penguin Books, New York, 1986).

_____, 'Introduction to an "Iconography of Medieval Architecture"' in *Studies in Early Christian, Medieval, and Renaissance Art* (New York University Press, New York, 1969).

_____, *Rome, Profile of a City, 312-1308* (Princeton University Press, Princeton, New Jersey, 1980).

_____, *Three Christian Capitals* (University of California Press, Berkeley, 1983).

Kretschmar, Georg, 'Die Geschichte des Taufgottesdienstes in der alten Kirche' in *Leiturgia* (Fünften Band. Johannes Stauda-Verlag Kassel, 1970).

Kuehn, Regina, *A Place for Baptism* (Liturgy Training Publications, Chicago, 1992).

Lamboglia, Nino, *Albenga, Romana e Medioevale,* 5 edizione (Istituto Internazionale di Studi Liguri, Albenga, Italy, 1981).

Lassus, Jean, 'Les baptistères africains' in *Corso di cultura sull' arte ravennate e bizantina* (Universita di Bologna, Bologna, 1970).

Leclercq, Henri, 'Baptistère' in *Dictionnaire d'archéologie chrétienne et de liturgie,* Tome Deuxieme. (Edited by Fernand Cabrol and Henri Leclercq) (Librairie Letouzey et Ané, Paris, 1925).

_____, 'Piscine' in *Dictionnaire d'archéologie chrétienne et de liturgie.* Tome Quatorzieme (Edited by Fernand Cabrol and Henri Leclercq) (Librairie Letouzey et Ané, Paris, 1939).

Ledwich, W., 'Baptism, Sacrament of the Cross, Looking behind St. Ambrose' in *The Sacrifice of Praise* (Edited by Bryan D. Spinks) (Edizioni Liturgiche, Rome, 1981).

Lézine, Alexandre, *Architecture romaine d'Afrique* (Presses Universitaires de France, Paris, 1961).

_____, *Thuburbo Maius* (Société Tunisienne de Diffusion, Tunis, 1968).

Lopreato, P. 'L'area di Piazza Capitolo e la domus sotto il battistero' in *Catalogue de l'exposition 'Aquileia romana'* (1991), pp.52-56.

Mahjoubi, Ammar, *Recherches d'histoire et d'archéologie a Henchir El-Faouar* (L'Universit de Tunis, Tunis, 1978).

Marchal, Michael G., and Rosemary G. Conrad, 'Womb and Tomb and Bath: A Temporary Baptismal Pool' in *Catechumenate,* 11:1 (January 1989), pp.31-34.

Mauck, Marchita, *Shaping a House for the Church* (Liturgy Training Publications, Chicago, 1990) Chapter 4: Initiation and Reconciliation.

Mazza, Enrico, *Mystagogy* (Pueblo Publishing Co., New York, 1989).

Milburn, Robert, *Early Christian Art and Architecture* (University of California Press, Berkeley, California, 1988) Chapter 12: Fonts and Baptisteries.

Mirabella Roberti, Mario, 'I battisteri dell'arco Adriatico' in *Antichita Altoadriatiche*, XIII (1978), pp.489-503.

_____, 'Il battistero antico di Milano' in *Ambrosius*, Supplement to No. 2 (1963).

_____, 'Il battistero di Castelseprio' in *Sibrium*, 16 (1982), pp.181-192.

_____, 'Il battistero di Sant' Ambrogio a Milano' in *Recherches augustiniennes*, IV (1966), pp.3-10.

_____, *Il battistero paleocristiano di Cividale* (Arti Grafiche Friulane, Udine, 1975).

_____, *Milano Romana* (Rusconi, Milano, 1984).

_____, and Angelo Paredi, *Il Battistero Ambrosiano di San Giovanni alle Fonti* (Veneranda Fabbrica del Duomo di Milano, Milano, n.d.).

Mitchell, Leonel L, 'Ambrosian Baptismal Rites' in *Studia Liturgica*, I:4 (1962), pp.241-253.

_____, 'The Thanksgiving over the Water in the Baptismal Rite of the Western Church' in Bryan D. Spinks (ed.) *The Sacrifice of Praise* (Edizioni Liturgiche, Rome, 1981).

Morey, C. R., The Origin of the Fish Symbol' in *Princeton Theological Review*. Part I: 8 (1910), pp.93-106, 231-246. Part II: 9 (1911), pp.268-289. Part III: 10 (1912), pp.278-298.

Mouchot, Danièle, *Nice-Cimiez, Le Musée d'Archèologie* (Action Culturelle Municipale, Nice, 1989).

Naissance des arts chrétiens (Atlas des monuments paléochrétiens de la France, Ministere de la Culture et de la Communication, Paris, 1991).

Nestori, A., 'Il battistero paleocristiana di S. Marcello: Nuovo scoperte' in *Rivista di archeologia cristiana*, 58:1 (1982), pp.81-119.

Nordström, Folke, *Mediaeval Baptismal Fonts, An Iconographical Study* (Umeå, Stockholm, 1984).

Nugent, Kenneth, 'Church Art and Architecture, New Life for an Old Church' in *The Clergy Review*, LXIX:10 (October 1984), pp.361-364.

Ofrasio, Timoteo Jose, *The Baptismal Font, A Study of Patristic and Liturgical Texts* (Pontificio Instituto Liturgico, Roma, 1990).

Palazzo, Eric, 'Iconographie et liturgie: la mosaique du baptistère de Kélibia (Tunisie)' in *Archiv fur Liturgiewissenschaft*, 34:1/2 (1992), pp.102-120.

Paley, F. A., *Illustrations of Baptismal Fonts* (John Van Voorst, London, 1844).

Paredi, Angelo, 'Il Battesimo nell'eta di S. Ambrogio' in *Il Battistero Ambrosiano di San Giovanni alle Fonti* (Veneranda Fabbrica del Duomo di Milano, Milano, n.d.).

Pellicioni, Giovanni, *Le Nuove Scoperte sulle Origini del Battistero Lateranense* (Tipographia Poliglotta Vaticana, Roma, 1973).

Perler, O., 'Die Taufsymbolik der vier Jahreszeiten im Baptisterium bei Kélibia' in *Mullus, Festschrift Th. Klauser* (Muenster, 1964), pp.282-290.

_____, L'inscription du baptistère de Saint-Thecle à Milan et le *De Sacramentis* de Saint Ambroise' in *Rivista di archeologia cristiana* (1951), pp.1-4.

Picard, Jean-Charles, 'Ce que les textes nous apprennent sur les équipements et le mobilier liturgique nécessaires pour le baptême: dans le Sud de la Gaule et l'Italie du nord' in *Actes du XIe congrès international d'archéologie chrétienne*, Vol. II (Lyon, Vienne, Grenoble, Genève et Aoste, 1986) (Pontificio Istituto di Archeologie Cristiana, Roma, 1989), pp.1451-1474.

————, 'L'archéologie chrétienne en Afrique 1938-1953' in *Actes du Ve congrès international d'archéologie chrétienne* (Aix-en-Provence, 1954). (Pontificio Istituto di Archeologie Cristiana, Roma, 1957), pp.45-59.

Reggiore, Ferdinando, *Dieci battisteri lombardi minori del secolo v-xii* (La Libreria dello Stato, Roma, 1935).

Reynaud, Jean-François, 'Le baptistère Saint-Etiene du groupe épiscopal de Lyon' in *Actes du Xe congrès international d'archéologie chrétienne*, Vol. II (Thessalonique, 1980) (Pontificio Istituto di Archeologia Cristiana, Roma, 1984), pp.463-475.

————, 'Le groupe épiscopal de Lyon, découvertes recentes' in *Comtes rendus des séances de l'Académie des Inscriptions et Belles-Lettres* (Novembre-Decembre 1975), pp.475-490.

————, *Lyon aux premiers temps chrétiens* (Ministere de la culture et de la communication, Paris, 1986).

Riley, Hugh M., *Christian Initiation: A Comparative Study of the Interpretation of the Baptismal Liturgy in the Mystagogical Writings of Cyril of Jerusalem, John Chrysostom, Theodore of Mopsuestia, and Ambrose of Milan* (The Catholic University of America Press, Washington, D. C., 1974).

Rogers, Clement F., *Baptism and Christian Archaeology* (Clarendon Press, Oxford, 1903).

Sant' Agostino nel Duomo di Milano (Nuove Edizioni Duomo, Milano, 1987).

Saxer, Victor, *Les rites de l'initiation chrétienne du IIe au VIe siecle* (Centro Italiano di Studi sull'alto Medioevo, Spoleto, 1988).

————, *Vie liturgique et quotidienne a Carthage vers le milieu du IIIe siecle* (Pontificio Istituto di Archeologia Cristiana, Roma, 1969).

Serra, Dominic, 'Portable Immersion Fonts' in *Chicago Catechumenate*, 6:1 (October 1983), pp.21-26.

Sironi, P. G. *Nuova guida di Castel Seprio* (1979).

Smith, E. Baldwin, *Early Christian Iconography* (Princeton Monographs in Art and Archaeology VI. Princeton University Press, Princeton, New Jersey, 1918).

————, *The Dome, A Study in the History of Ideas* (Princeton University Press, Princeton, New Jersey, 1950).

Sordi, Marta, *et al.*, *Agostino a Milano, Il Battesimo* (Palermo, Edizioni Augustinus, 1988).

Srawley, J. H., ed., *St. Ambrose, On the Sacraments and On the Mysteries* (SPCK, Second edition, London, 1950).

Stauffer, S. Anita, 'A Place for Burial, Birth and Bath, The Font as Symbol' in *Liturgy*, 5:4 (Spring 1986), pp.51-57.

————, 'Cultural Settings of Architecture for Baptism in the Early Church' in *Worship and Culture in Dialogue* (Lutheran World Federation, Geneva, Switzerland, 1994).

————, 'Fonts, Baptism, Pascha, and Paradise' in *Studia Liturgica*, 24:1 (1994), pp.58-65.

————, 'Fonts for Function and Meaning, Three Worthy Examples' in *Catechumenate*, 10:2 (March 1988), pp.22-29.

————, 'Lessons from the Baptism of Augustine' in *Lutheran Forum*, 21:2 (1989), pp.16-17.

————, *Re-examining Baptismal Fonts* (Videotape) (Liturgical Press, Collegeville, Minnesota, 1991).

Stern, H., 'Le décor des pavements et des cuves dans les baptistères paléochrétiens' in *Actes du Ve congrès international d'archéologie chrétienne* (Aix-en-Provence, 1954) (Pontificio Istituto di Archeologia Cristiana, Roma, 1957), pp.381-390.

Stevick, Daniel B. *Baptismal Moments; Baptismal Meanings* (Church Hymnal Corporation, New York, 1987).

Stommel, Eduard, 'Christliche Taufriten und antike Badesitten' in *Jahrbuch fur Antike und Christentum*, 2 (1959), pp.5-14.

Swift, Emerson H., *Roman Sources of Christian Art* (Columbia University Press, New York, 1951.

Tamaro, Bruna Forlati, *et al.*,, *Da Aquileia a Venezia, Una mediazione tra l'Europa e l'Oriente dal II secolo a. C. al VI secolo d. C.* (Libri Scheiwiller, Milano, 1980).

Tavano, Sergio, *Aquileia, Guida dei Monumenti Cristiani* (Arti Grafiche Friulane, Udine, Italy, 1984).

Thomas, Charles, *Christianity in Roman Britain to AD 500* (B. T. Batsford, London, 1985) Chapter 8: Baptism and Baptisteries.

Traversari, G., *Architettura paleocristiana milanese* (Milano, 1964).

Tunisie, (Hatchette guides bleus, Paris, 1987—Archaeological site notes by Noel Duval.)

Tyrell-Green, E., *Baptismal Fonts Classified and Illustrated* (SPCK, London, 1928).

Underwood, Paul A, 'The Fountain of Life in Manuscripts of the Gospels' in *Dumbarton Oaks Papers*, No. 5 (Harvard University Press, Cambridge, Massachusetts, 1950).

Van Dael, Peter, 'Purpose and Function of Decoration-Schemes in Early Christian Baptisteries' in *Fides Sacramenti, Sacramentum Fidei* (Van Gordum Assen, Netherlands, 1981).

Van der Meer, F., *Augustine the Bishop, Religion and Society at the Dawn of the Middle Ages* (Sheed and Ward, London, 1961).

————, *Early Christian Art* (Faber and Faber Ltd., London, 1967).

————, and Mohrmann, Christine, *Atlas of the Early Christian World* (Nelson, New York, 1958).

Vaultrin, J., 'Les basiliques chrétiennes de Carthage' in *Revue africaine*, LXX (1932).

Verzone, Paolo, *L'architettura religiosa dell' alto medio evo nell' Italia settentrionale* (Officine Grafiche Esperia, Milano, 1942).

Wall, J. Charles, *Porches and Fonts* (Wells Gardner, Darton & Co. Ltd., London, 1912).

Wehrhahn-Stauch, Liselotte, 'Christliche Fischsymbolik von den Anfängen bis zum hohen mittelalter' in *Zeitschrift für Kunstgeschichte* (Deutscher Kunstverlag, München, 1972).

Wharton, Annabel Jane, 'Ritual and Reconstructed Meaning: The Neonian Baptistery in Ravenna' in *The Art Bulletin*, LXIX:3 (September 1987), pp.358-375.

Whitaker, E. C., *Documents of the Baptismal Liturgy* (Second edition, revised, SPCK, London, 1970).

Windfeld-Hansen, H., 'Edifices antiques a plan central d'apres les architectes de la renaissance et baptistères paléochrétiens' in *Actes du Ve congrès international d'archéologie chrétienne* (Aix-en-Provence, 1954) (Pontificio Istituto di Archeologie Cristiana, Roma, 1957), pp.391-399.

Yacoub, Mohamed, *Chefs-d'oeuvre des musées nationaux de Tunisie* (Maison Tunisiene de l'Edition, Tunis, 1978).

———, *Le musée du Bardo* (Ministere des Affaires Culturelles, Tunis, 1970).

Yarnold, Edward, *The Awe-Inspiring Rites of Initiation: Baptismal Homilies of the Fourth Century* (St. Paul Publications, Slough, England, 1971).

———, *The Awe-Inspiring Rites of Initiation: The Origins of The Rite of Christian Initiation of Adults* (second edition, T. & T. Clark, Edinburgh, 1994).

Zovatto, Paolo Lino, *Grado, Antichi Monumenti* (Calderini, Grado, 1971).

———, 'Il Battistero di Grado' in *Rivista di archeologia cristiana*, 23-24:1-4 (1947-1948), pp.231-251.

Index

THE GROUP FOR RENEWAL OF WORSHIP (GROW)

This Group, originally founded in 1961, has for well over twenty years taken responsiblity for the Grove Books publications on liturgy and worship. Its membership and broad aims reflect a highly reforming, pastoral and missionary interest in worship. Beginning with a youthful evangelical Anglican membership in the early 1970s, the Group has not only probed adventurously into the future of Anglican worship, but has also with growing sureness of touch taken its place in promoting weighty scholarship. Thus the list of 'Grove Liturgical Studies' (published on page 76 overleaf) shows how, over a twelve-year period, the quarterly Studies added steadily to the material available to students of patristic, reformation and modern scholarly issues in liturgy. In 1986 the Group was approached by the Alcuin Club Committee with a view to publishing the new series of Joint Liturgical Studies, and this series is, at the time of writing, in its eighth year of publication, sustaining the programme with three Studies each year.

Between the old Grove Liturgical Studies and the new Joint Liturgical Studies there is a large provision of both English language texts and other theological works on the patristic era. A detailed list is available from the publishers.

Since the early 1970s the Group has had Colin Buchanan as chairman and Trevor Lloyd as vice-chairman.

THE ALCUIN CLUB

The Alcuin Club exists to promote the study of Christian liturgy in general, and in particular the liturgies of the Anglican Communion. Since its foundation in 1897 it has published over 130 books and pamphlets. Members of the Club receive some publications of the current year free and others at a reduced rate.

Information concerning the annual subscription, applications for membership and lists of publications is obtainable from the Treasurer, The Revd. T. R. Barker, 11 Abbey Street, Chester CH1 2JF. (Tel. 0244 347811, Fax 0244 347823).

The Alcuin Club has a three-year arrangement with the Liturgical Press, Collegeville, whereby the old tradition of an annual Alcuin Club major scholarly study has been restored. The first title under this arrangement was published in early 1993: Alastair McGregor, *Fire and Light: The Symbolism of Fire and Light in the Holy Week Services.*

The Joint Liturgical Studies have been reduced to three per annum from 1992, and the Alcuin Club subscription now includes the annual publication (as above) and the three Joint Liturgical Studies (with an extra in 1994). The full list of Joint Liturgical Studies is printed opposite. All titles are in print.

Alcuin/GROW Joint Liturgical Studies

All cost £3.95 (US $8) in 1994

Grove Liturgical Studies

This series began in March 1975, and was published quarterly until 1986. Each title has 32 or 40 pages. Nos. 1, 3-6, 9, 10, 44 and 46 are out of print. Asterisked numbers have been reprinted. Prices in 1994, £2.75.